HAWAIIAN ISLANDS
(SANDWICH ISLANDS)

Niihau · Kauai · Oahu · Maui
Kealakekua Bay · Hawaii

PACIFIC OCEAN

EQUATOR

MARQUESAS
ISLANDS

Rakahanga
(Peregrina)

Tahuata

Taumako

SANTA CRUZ ISLANDS

POLYNESIA

Leper Island
Aurora
Pentecost

NEW HEBRIDES
(GREAT CYCLADES)

Erromanga
Tanna

W CALEDONIA

HOORN ISLANDS

FIJI

SAMOA ISLANDS

FRIENDLY
ISLANDS

Niue

Tongatabu
(Amsterdam)

TONGA

Eua (Middleburg)

Palmerston Atoll

COOK ISLANDS

HERVEY ISLAND

Rarotonga

PALLISER ISLANDS

SOCIETY ISLANDS

Rajatea

Huahine

Mopihaa

Moorea
(Eimeo)

Tahiti
(King George III
Island)

TUAMOTU ISLANDS

Pitcairn Island

Norfolk Island

THREE KINGS
ISLANDS

Cape Maria
van Diemen

NEW
ZEALAND

Queen Charlotte's
Sound

Cape
Farewell

Tolaga Bay

Young Nick's Head

NORTH ISLAND

Cook Strait

Southern Alps

SOUTH ISLAND

Sound

THE PACIFIC NAVIGATORS

The Seafarers THE PACIFIC
NAVIGATORS

Other Publications:

THE EPIC OF FLIGHT
THE GOOD COOK
THE ENCYCLOPEDIA OF COLLECTIBLES
THE GREAT CITIES
WORLD WAR II
HOME REPAIR AND IMPROVEMENT
THE WORLD'S WILD PLACES
THE TIME-LIFE LIBRARY OF BOATING
HUMAN BEHAVIOR
THE ART OF SEWING
THE OLD WEST
THE EMERGENCE OF MAN
THE AMERICAN WILDERNESS
THE TIME-LIFE ENCYCLOPEDIA OF GARDENING
LIFE LIBRARY OF PHOTOGRAPHY
THIS FABULOUS CENTURY
FOODS OF THE WORLD
TIME-LIFE LIBRARY OF AMERICA
TIME-LIFE LIBRARY OF ART
GREAT AGES OF MAN
LIFE SCIENCE LIBRARY
THE LIFE HISTORY OF THE UNITED STATES
TIME READING PROGRAM
LIFE NATURE LIBRARY
LIFE WORLD LIBRARY
FAMILY LIBRARY:
   HOW THINGS WORK IN YOUR HOME
   THE TIME-LIFE BOOK OF THE FAMILY CAR
   THE TIME-LIFE FAMILY LEGAL GUIDE
   THE TIME-LIFE BOOK OF FAMILY FINANCE

The Cover: In this painting by William
Hodges, the ships of Britain's James Cook
—the greatest Pacific navigator—
anchor in Tahiti's Matavai Bay in 1773.
Another British expedition had
found Tahiti six years earlier during a
circumnavigation of the globe.

The Title Page: This ebony-handled
brass sextant belonged to French
explorer Louis Antoine de Bougainville,
who crossed the Pacific in the late
1760s. His reports of Polynesian societies
helped establish the European idea
of the South Seas as an earthly paradise.

The Seafarers

THE PACIFIC NAVIGATORS

by Oliver E. Allen
AND THE EDITORS OF TIME-LIFE BOOKS

TIME-LIFE BOOKS, ALEXANDRIA, VIRGINIA

Time-Life Books Inc.
is a wholly owned subsidiary of
TIME INCORPORATED

FOUNDER: Henry R. Luce 1898-1967

Editor-in-Chief: Henry Anatole Grunwald
President: J. Richard Munro
Chairman of the Board: Ralph P. Davidson
Executive Vice President: Clifford J. Grum
Editorial Director: Ralph Graves
Vice Chairman: Arthur Temple

TIME-LIFE BOOKS INC.

MANAGING EDITOR: Jerry Korn
Executive Editor: David Maness
Assistant Managing Editors: Dale M. Brown (planning),
George Constable, Thomas H. Flaherty Jr. (acting),
Martin Mann, John Paul Porter
Art Director: Tom Suzuki
Chief of Research: David L. Harrison
Director of Photography: Robert G. Mason
Assistant Art Director: Arnold C. Holeywell
Assistant Chief of Research: Carolyn L. Sackett
Assistant Director of Photography: Dolores A. Littles

CHAIRMAN: Joan D. Manley
President: John D. McSweeney
Executive Vice Presidents: Carl G. Jaeger,
John Steven Maxwell, David J. Walsh
Vice Presidents: George Artandi (comptroller);
Stephen L. Bair (legal counsel); Peter G. Barnes;
Nicholas Benton (public relations); John L. Canova;
Beatrice T. Dobie (personnel); Carol Flaumenhaft
(consumer affairs); James L. Mercer
(Europe/South Pacific); Herbert Sorkin (production);
Paul R. Stewart (marketing)

The Seafarers

Editorial Staff for The Pacific Navigators:
Editor: Jim Hicks
Designer: Herbert H. Quarmby
Chief Researcher: W. Mark Hamilton
Picture Editor: John Conrad Weiser
Text Editors: Anne Horan, Stuart Gannes, Gus Hedberg,
Lydia Preston
Staff Writers: Kathleen M. Burke, Kumait N. Jawdat,
David Thiemann
Researchers: Barbara Brownell, Mindy A. Daniels,
Roxie M. France, Philip Brandt George, Fran Glennon,
Sheila M. Green, Ann Dusel Kuhns, Kimberly Lewis
Art Assistant: Michelle René Clay
Editorial Assistant: Ellen Keir

Special Contributors
David S. Thomson (essays); Martha Reichard George,
Barbara Hicks (research)

Editorial Production
Production Editor: Douglas B. Graham
Operations Manager: Gennaro C. Esposito,
Gordon E. Buck (assistant)
Assistant Production Editor: Feliciano Madrid
Quality Control: Robert L. Young (director), James J. Cox
(assistant), Daniel J. McSweeney, Michael G. Wight (associates)
Art Coordinator: Anne B. Landry
Copy Staff: Susan B. Galloway (chief), Anne T. Connell,
Sheirazada Hann, Celia Beattie
Picture Department: Jane Martin
Traffic: Jeanne Potter

Correspondents: Elisabeth Kraemer (Bonn); Margot
Hapgood, Dorothy Bacon, Lesley Coleman (London);
Susan Jonas, Lucy T. Voulgaris (New York); Maria
Vincenza Aloisi, Josephine du Brusle (Paris); Ann
Natanson (Rome).
Valuable assistance was provided by Nakanori Tashiro,
Asia Editor, Tokyo. The editors also wish to thank: Janny
Hovinga (Amsterdam); Enid Farmer (Boston); Sandy
Jacobi, Katrina Van Duyn (Copenhagen); Karen Horton,
Tom Kaser (Honolulu); Tomas Loayza (Lima); Judy
Aspinall (London); Janet Zich (Los Angeles); Jane Walker
(Madrid); Douglas Tunstell (Málaga); John Dunn
(Melbourne); Carolyn T. Chubet, Miriam Hsia, Christina
Lieberman (New York); Al Prince (Papeete); Mimi
Murphy (Rome); Peter Allen (Sydney).

The Author:
Oliver E. Allen first saw the South Pacific
from a troop carrier during World War II,
when he was a U.S. Army sergeant on his
way to New Guinea. He is a former mem-
ber of the staff of Time-Life Books, where
he served as editor of two series, the LIFE
World Library and the TIME-LIFE Library of
America, and also as planning director.
Now a full-time writer, he lives in Pelham,
New York. His published works include
The Windjammers in The Seafarers series.

The Consultants:
John Horace Parry, Gardiner Professor of
Oceanic History and Affairs at Harvard
University, served as a commander in the
Royal Navy during World War II. He is the
author of many distinguished historical
studies, including Trade and Dominion
and The Discovery of the Sea.

Ben R. Finney, Professor of Anthropology
at the University of Hawaii, earned his
Ph.D. at Harvard University. A specialist
in prehistoric Pacific migration, he sailed
in a reconstructed Polynesian canoe on a
round-trip voyage between Hawaii and Tahiti. The journey is described in his book
Hokule'a: The Way to Tahiti.

David Lyon, educated at King's College,
Cambridge, has participated in underwater
surveys of 18th Century ships and is an authority on historical ships' plans. He is a
member of the board of the Nautical Ar-
chaeological Trust.

For information about any Time-Life book, please write:
Reader Information, Time-Life Books,
541 North Fairbanks Court, Chicago, Illinois 60611.

TIME-LIFE is a trademark of Time Incorporated U.S.A.

Library of Congress Cataloguing in Publication Data
Allen, Oliver E
    The Pacific navigators.
    (The Seafarers)
    Bibliography: p.
    Includes index.
    1. Oceanica—Discovery and exploration. 2. Tasman,
Abel Janszoon, 1603?-1659. 3. Bougainville, Louis
Antoine de, Comte, 1729-1811. 4. Cook, James, 1728-
1779. 5. Explorers—Oceanica—Biography. I. Time-
Life Books. II. Title. III. Series: Seafarers.
DU20.A55   910'.92'2   80-13963
ISBN 0-8094-2687-0
ISBN 0-8094-2686-2 lib. bdg.
ISBN 0-8094-2685-4 retail Ed.

Contents

New Edens in the South Seas

The European navigators who first dared investigate the immensity of the Pacific Ocean found there a world that was as enchanting as it was surprising. With its scattered islands and archipelagoes of alien landscapes—low-lying atolls and majestic fjords, lush green foliage and luminous atmosphere—it was different from anything Europeans had seen before. What was more, it was a world whose inhabitants often seemed to possess an innocence belonging to an earlier age of mankind. "I thought I was transported into the Garden of Eden," exclaimed French mariner Louis de Bougainville when he visited Tahiti in 1768.

Bold voyagers like Bougainville ranged the Pacific over a 200-year period between the mid-16th and mid-18th Centuries—and in the process they composed many a rapturous account for reading back home. Yet they produced little pictorial evidence of how these wondrous places looked until an obscure landscape painter named William Hodges was appointed by the Admiralty to accompany Captain James Cook on a British expedition that set out in 1772.

Hodges himself derived little lasting benefit from this opportunity; despite a gust of glory after his return with Cook, he failed in the cutthroat world of London art and died penniless—probably a suicide—in 1797. But the products of his maritime meanderings were unique. In paintings like those shown here and on the following pages, he retraced the paths along which Spanish, Dutch, French and English mariners probed the great ocean between 1565, when Don Alvaro de Mendaña pioneered the movement from the Spanish frontier in Peru, and 1775, when Cook's second voyage brought the era to its zenith.

Paddlers in canoes round a rocky headland, in Hodges' oil of Tahuata, one of the Marquesas, where a Spanish expedition had anchored in 1595.

A Maori family stands beside a rainbow-graced cascade that falls into Dusky Bay, New Zealand, visited by Dutch explorer Abel Tasman in 1642.

Against a backdrop of volcanic peaks and coconut palms, island women bathe in a bay at Tahiti, first visited by the English and French in the 1760s.

Storm clouds build behind towering statues on Easter Island. The skull in the foreground symbolizes the death of the civilization that carved them.

Chapter 1
First probes for a chimerical continent

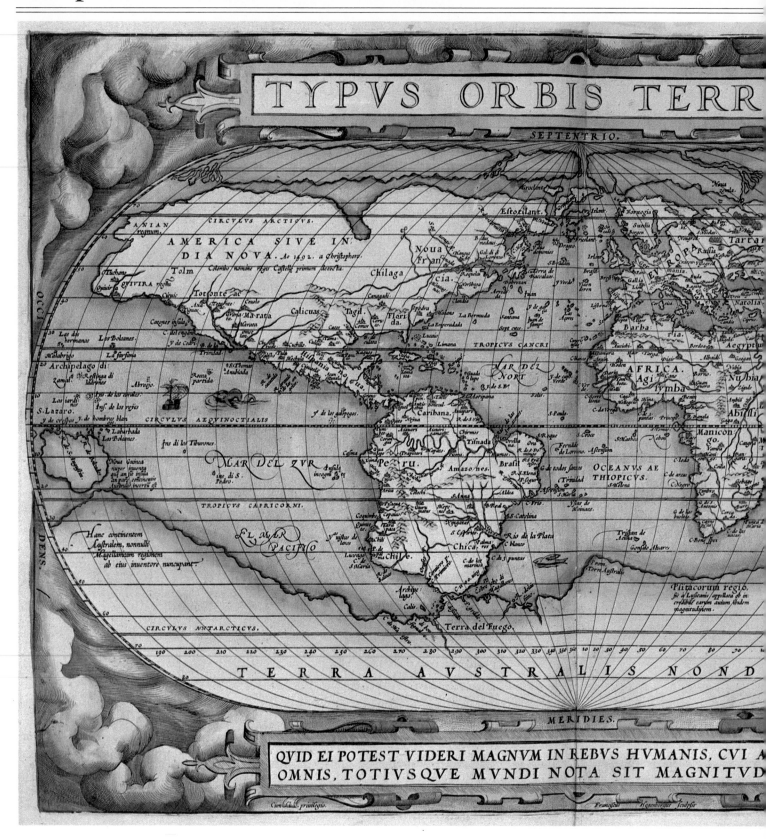

The vast expanse of a supposed continent—called Terra Australis Nondum Cognita, the "southern land not yet known"—girdles the bottom of the world on this 1570 map. Beginning in the 16th Century, European navigators spent 200 years looking for the fabled land mass, whose existence had first been postulated by the ancient Greeks.

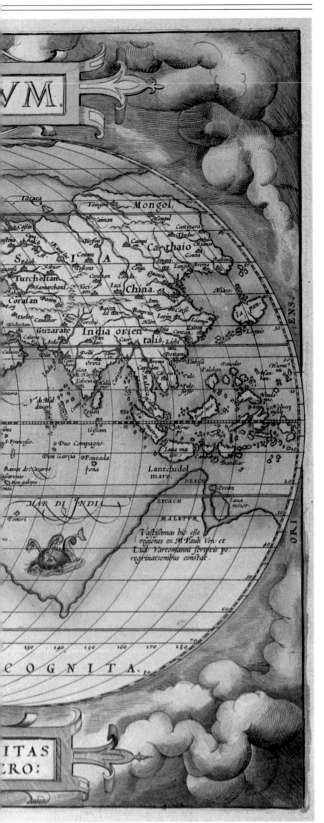

hen Spanish conquistadors overran Peru in the 16th Century, Inca dwelling in the Andean highlands told them a tale of a pair of wondrous islands lying to the west, somewhere in the vastness of the Pacific Ocean. As the Indians recounted it, Tupac Yupanqui, a great 15th Century Inca ruler, had made his way there with a fleet of reed vessels and 20,000 warriors. He returned with a haul that reflected the islands' wealth—a gleaming brass throne, the hide of a horse, a corps of black retainers—and he spoke glowingly of fertile fields and lordly mountains, abundant gold, and a docile people eager to do his bidding. To the 16th Century Inca, the tale offered a wistful counterweight against their present miseries at the hands of the Spaniards. To Spanish colonial officers, it was an invitation to further conquest and adventure.

No one was more fascinated by the story than a gentleman-warrior named Pedro Sarmiento de Gamboa, a scholarly eccentric who spent his leisure hours learning the Inca language and lore. As a man of considerable erudition, Sarmiento was predisposed to accept the report of the Inca discovery; it conveniently dovetailed with a geographical theory that Western savants had been postulating for more than 1,000 years. In the Second Century A.D. the great Greek astronomer Claudius Ptolemy, believing that the earth must be balanced lest it topple over, had concluded that somewhere below the Indian Ocean lay a land mass roughly equal in size to Europe and Asia. Over the centuries the hypothetical existence of such a continent—called *Terra Australis Incognita*, "unknown southern land"—had hardened into intellectual dogma.

In the century just before Sarmiento's time, European explorers had expanded the map of the known world almost exponentially. Portuguese seafarers led by Vasco da Gama had revealed the outlines of Africa, the East Indies and the north coast of New Guinea; Christopher Columbus had found the Americas; and Ferdinand Magellan had circumnavigated the globe. Now that Spain had established an empire in the Americas, Spanish galleons were beginning to ply a track between Mexico and the Philippines. But south of that track the Pacific remained a blank. "Land here is certain," wrote the 16th Century Flemish cartographer Gerard Mercator across one of his maps, "but how much and to what limits is uncertain."

Sarmiento had no reason not to assume that the fabled Inca islands lay near the Terra Australis Incognita of Ptolemaic belief—and every reason for trying to find both the islands and the continent from Peru. In 1567 he persuaded the Viceroy of Peru to authorize an expedition in search of the promised lands. He thus inaugurated a quest that would engross venturesome navigators for more than two centuries.

The men who joined this quest traveled astonishing distances, endured incredible hardships and demonstrated heroic courage. The Pacific stretches as far as 10,000 miles from east to west and 10,000 from north to south. To guide them across this immensity, the early voyagers had only the crudest of navigational instruments: the astrolabe—a device that ascertained latitude by the position of the sun or stars—and the compass. Not until the mid-18th Century did anyone develop a means for accurately determining longitude at sea. Until then, Pacific navigators were never sure precisely how far west or east they had traveled from home, or how far they were from their goal.

Yet with all those odds against them, hundreds of European navigators set forth upon the Pacific between the 1560s and the 1780s. They went out in successive waves, under four different flags and with incentives that changed with the times. Sarmiento and his fellow Spaniards began the quest with a lusty zeal that entwined finding gold with serving God and the Spanish Empire. The Dutch took up the search in the 17th Century in a more prosaic spirit, seeking trade. In the 18th Century came the French, looking for markets not yet claimed by the Dutch but finding romance and fare for ruminations on the nature of human society. The English, succeeding the French, brought to the enterprise scientific research and the pursuit of knowledge for its own sake.

None of them found the great Southern land mass of Ptolemy's imaginings, nor the paradise of the Inca. But together they gradually defined the continent later known as Australia—which, in its expanse of nearly three million square miles, was tremendous enough in itself—and the thousands of islands scattered about the sea. In so doing they filled in the last major blanks in the map of the habitable world.

Of all the expeditions that ventured into the Pacific in those 200 years, few set forth with more forbidding prospects than did the one initiated by Sarmiento in 1567. The Peruvian Viceroy, Lope García de Castro, provided two square-rigged ships—the 250-ton *Los Reyes* and the *Todos Santos*, 107 tons—and a company of 150 men, including 70 soldiers, three or four pilots, a purser, four Franciscan friars and a number of black slaves. But the ships were not built to withstand weather any more severe than that normally expected in the benign waters along the Peruvian coast. And the Viceroy's command appointments were certain to cause friction.

Sarmiento, having proposed the voyage, assumed he would lead it. He saw himself as the spiritual heir of Cortés and Pizarro, conquerors of Mexico and Peru. But García de Castro had his own dreams of glory, and he gave command of the expedition to a kinsman, a 25-year-old nephew named Alvaro de Mendaña de Neyra. Sarmiento had to settle for the rank of second-in-command and captaincy of the *Todos Santos*.

The youthful Mendaña, who knew nothing whatever of the sea, was a gentle, patient and earnest young man—but he seldom made up his mind without consulting all those around him. Quite naturally, the one to whom he regularly turned for advice at sea was the chief pilot, Hernán Gallego, an experienced man who had been piloting vessels since the age of 15. Now a decisive, crusty seaman in his fifties, Gallego paid no heed to Sarmiento's opinions about navigation, thus fanning conflict between Sarmiento and himself and between Sarmiento and Mendaña.

The ships sailed on a west-by-southwest course from Callao, Peru's chief seaport, on November 19, 1567—the feast day of Saint Isabel, whom the voyagers named patroness of the expedition. On December 4, after they had reached 15° 30′ S., the lookout sighted a cloud bank on the horizon. Sarmiento eagerly concluded that it must be hovering over the fabled Inca islands and proposed that the ships head directly for it. But

A mariner points the indicator on an astrolabe at the sun to determine his latitude. Originally a complex instrument for astronomers, the astrolabe was simplified for navigational use in the 15th Century and was weighted to keep it vertical on a pitching ship.

Another mariner figures latitude by sighting along a cross-staff to read the sun's altitude—a risky process that could damage his eyes. But the cross-staff could fix latitude to within about one degree of accuracy, while the astrolabe sometimes erred up to five degrees.

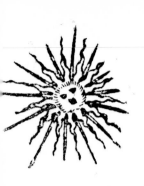

Gallego declared it meant nothing and refused to change course, and Mendaña agreed. Sarmiento was furious, stating in his diary that Gallego had "missed the discovery." (There is in fact no land there.)

On January 15, after almost two months at sea, a pleasant-looking island came into view, and a number of its inhabitants paddled out in canoes and waved cordially. The Spaniards' hopes rose. But before they could anchor, wind and current combined to carry the ships away, and they could not beat their way back. Morale sank.

Another two weeks passed, and at last on February 7, 1568, after 80 days at sea, the lookout spied what appeared to be an extensive body of land about 50 miles to the southwest. "We hoisted a flag, and everybody received the news with great joy and gratitude," wrote Gallego. "We all prayed, singing the *Te Deum laudamus.*"

The island they were nearing was a volcanic prominence graced with palm trees and lush vegetation. "As it was so large and high," Mendaña recalled, "we thought it must be a continent"—surely Terra Australis Incognita. Gallego estimated in the ship's log that they had come about 6,000 miles. Actually, he had underestimated by more than 2,000 miles; he was not aware that the swift-running currents of the open Pacific had moved the ships about a third again as rapidly as they would have traveled under wind power alone. Gallego's error was of no particular moment just then, but it would remain in the record and would confound navigators who came after him.

As the Spanish vessels approached the shore, a flotilla of crescent-shaped canoes came out to meet them. The people in the canoes were almost completely naked. Some were dark-skinned, others lighter; most had curly hair. At first glance they resembled the Indians of Peru, so the Spaniards called these people Indians too.

These islanders made friendly signs and, calling up to the Spaniards crowding the rails, asked for the *tabriqui*, which Mendaña correctly interpreted as meaning "chief." He identified himself and threw down a red hat, one of a number of trifles the Spaniards had brought along as presents. A man who appeared to be the local *tabriqui* seized it eagerly and put it on. Mendaña invited him and some others to come on board, cordially embraced them, gave them food, and handed out red hats, bells and beads all around.

The inhabitants took this display of generosity as an indication that they were welcome to anything. Soon they were scampering all over the ship, picking up loose objects that caught their fancy and tossing them overboard to companions who had remained in the canoes below. To the great amusement of the Spaniards, one islander climbed briskly to the top of the rigging, undaunted by the height or the sway. Good-natured at first, the crewmen eventually wearied of their visitors' antics and shouted "*Afuera! Afuera!*" ("Away! Away!"). The islanders seemed to understand, for although they shouted back the same word, they departed.

The Spaniards waited until the next day before they brought the ships inshore and anchored them in a bay. As they did so, one of the men noticed that a surprisingly bright star was shining in the morning light. "We took it for a guide," Gallego later recalled, "and grew cheerful and full of hope." In remembrance of the moment, they called the harbor

Bahía de la Estrella (Bay of the Star). And they named the land Santa Isabel, after the patroness of their voyage. Going ashore, Mendaña took possession of the island in the name of the King of Spain. The Franciscan friars erected a cross and chanted the hymn *Vexilla Regis Prodeunt*— "Abroad the Regal Banners Fly."

A party under Gallego immediately started felling trees to build a launch for exploring the coastline. The rest of the company returned to the ships. The next day a canoe came out. In it sat another chieftain— this one evidently more elevated than the *tabriqui* of the day before, for he wore an elaborate headdress of black and white plumes and armlets made of shell and was attended by a sizable retinue. He gave his name as Bilebanara. Amiably gesticulating and parroting the visitors' words, he promised to supply food to supplement the now-moldering meat and biscuit the Spaniards had brought from home.

Two days passed, but Bilebanara delivered no food. Growing uneasy, Mendaña decided to send Sarmiento ashore with a reconnoitering party. He told the men to behave humanely and cause no trouble, to barter for what they needed, and to use their weapons only in self-defense.

They landed and penetrated about a dozen miles into a thick forest, but found little in the way of food before they paused for the night. They had no sooner made camp than snipers began shooting arrows at them; no one was hit, and mindful of Mendaña's instructions, the Spaniards frightened away their attackers by firing harquebuses into the air. During the night there was a heavy rainstorm, and in the morning— drenched and dispirited—they decided to give up and return to the ship. As they headed toward the beach, they were attacked by a band of warriors shooting arrows and throwing stones—and shouting, aptly, "*Afuera!*" One of Sarmiento's soldiers was wounded by an arrow, and the Spanish fired back in earnest, hitting several of their attackers and seriously wounding one. Sarmiento finished that victim off with his sword. The slain man was the first of a long list of South Sea casualties that visiting Europeans would leave in their wake.

Unrepentant, the Spaniards set off on a second and bigger mission a few days later. This time they went farther inland and, in high excitement, climbed to the top of a ridge, hoping to find the riches of Terra Australis Incognita laid out before them. But the vantage revealed no panorama of rolling fields studded with gold temples; instead, they saw more trees and, in the distance, another shoreline—disappointing evidence that Santa Isabel was only an island. As they dejectedly descended the slope they had climbed, they were pursued once more by men who materialized out of the bush, and by the time they regained the beach they were bloodied and angry.

By April, after nearly two months of skirmishes, the Spaniards were thoroughly disenchanted with the island. Mendaña was not yet ready to leave for home, however. The ships' carpenters had completed a shallow-draft launch, an undecked vessel of four or five tons, with a single sail and a flat bottom that made her ideal for island-hopping. On April 7 Mendaña sent the launch off with a party of 22 men under Gallego's pilotage to explore nearby waters for a more promising land.

After about two weeks' sailing through what they now realized was a

Lope García de Castro, the Viceroy of Peru who in 1567 subsidized the first Spanish expedition to explore the Pacific, had authorized a similar venture two years earlier, but canceled it after he learned that the crew was planning to seize the ship in order to pursue a more lucrative enterprise: piracy.

chain of islands, the explorers decided to stop at one that appeared to be worthy of investigation. The shore had a fine harbor that was free of reefs. A broad savanna reached inland, looking fit for agriculture and cattle raising. A good river coursed down from a distant mountain. The Spaniards found some inhabitants and, hearing the name of the place in the alien tongue, tried to imitate the sound—but corrupted it into Guadalcanal, the name of a town they knew in Spain.

Guadalcanal held more than agricultural promise. Among the expedition's company were a number of men who had experience in the Peruvian gold mines, and Gallego later recalled: "The miners, who understand the thing, said that there was gold in the land." So the Spaniards made their way back to Estrella Bay and persuaded Mendaña to transfer the base to the newly discovered land. On May 12 the two ships followed the launch to Guadalcanal.

The Spaniards ceremoniously claimed possession, planting a cross and reading prayers in honor of their King. Mendaña then dispatched one party into the woods to prospect for gold and another to look for food. The gold seekers had no sooner begun to pan the river than "so many natives annoyed them that they were obliged to abandon the attempt," said Gallego. The men looking for food had no better luck. The islanders "kept on shouting and sounding their conchs and horns, giving the war cry," recalled one of the officers. But instead of making an effort to appease the inhabitants, the Spaniards rashly captured a small boy, intending to use him as a hostage to trade for food. When a man came to claim the child—who was his son—and offered only a pig in exchange, the Spaniards indignantly seized the pig but refused to give up the boy. He remained with them throughout the voyage and was taken back to Lima, there to disappear from history.

The Spaniards' callousness was soon repaid. On May 26 a watering party of 10 men was set upon by warriors, who killed nine of the explorers. The lone survivor swam to the safety of the ships and reported that the islanders had cut his fellows "into pieces, taking out their tongues and sucking out their brains with great ferocity." Mendaña rushed ashore with intentions of restoring peace, only to find that the warriors were gleefully waving dismembered limbs at him and hoisting flags made from the victims' clothes. More islanders were streaming down from the hills. "It was something to hear the clamor and noise that the Indians made with their drums," Gallego wrote. "It seemed as if it were a day of gathering for judgment." Mendaña's party retreated to the ships.

After another month and a half of frustrated attempts to reach a rapprochement with the inhabitants—here, and on several other neighboring islands—the Spaniards decided the time had come to reappraise the situation. No continent had been found, and colonization of these islands seemed less likely every day. The supply of food they had brought from home was running low; so was ammunition. Mendaña summoned the company to discuss the next step. First he outlined his own views. The mission had been to find a new continent; he was in favor of resuming the search, sailing south to lat. 20° or 22° to see what was there.

Gallego, volunteering his opinion next, agreed that the hostility of the islanders ruled out staying. But he reminded Mendaña that the ships

were leaky and that their rigging was deteriorating. Even if the Southern continent existed, there was no guarantee that they could reach it. He proposed that the expedition give up the quest and sail home forthwith.

The friars spoke next. They said the best plan would be to set a course for New Guinea, which—taking a wild guess—they thought was nearer than Peru; from there it would be easy to find Manila, where they could count on kindred Spanish colonists for aid.

The last to speak was Pedro Sarmiento—and he disagreed with everybody. As a soldier, he argued that there was nothing to fear from the islanders: The Spanish force was sufficiently strong to put down any attack. He urged staying in the islands and getting on with the business of prospecting for gold.

But Sarmiento stood practically alone. The sentiment of the company generally favored a direct return to Peru, whatever the distance. Mendaña ordered the ships made ready for sailing as soon as possible. Sarmiento never forgave him.

They sailed before dawn on the morning of August 11, a good wind briskly carrying them off to the northeast. On August 18, 1568, the Spaniards had their last look at the island chain they had discovered. The islands would not be seen again by Europeans for another 200 years.

A map drawn soon after Magellan discovered a passage between the tip of South America and Tierra del Fuego in 1520 depicts the route as wide and easy. In fact, the Strait of Magellan is a treacherous labyrinth of narrow, cliff-bound channels churned by waves that are 40 feet high, and it proved a dangerous obstacle course for most of the Pacific explorers who traversed it.

A new round of calamities now awaited Mendaña and his party. At the very outset of the homeward passage it became apparent that the *Todos Santos*, the leakier of the two ships, could not keep up with the flagship *Los Reyes*; every day she slipped farther behind, and on October 16 she vanished over the horizon. Since Sarmiento was captain of the *Todos Santos*, Mendaña leaped to the conclusion that his truculent second-in-command had deliberately gone off on his own. Mendaña was pondering whether or not to go in search of the *Todos Santos* when a hurricane struck. "The wind came on us with such fury," Gallego later wrote, "as I have never before seen, although I have been 45 years at sea." The stern cabin was carried away and the hull flooded, causing the ship to roll over on her side. For a day and a half she wallowed helplessly in the roaring seas. By the time the storm had abated and the crew could pump her out, Mendaña and Gallego had concluded that the *Todos Santos* was irretrievably lost. They decided to press on without her.

But the flagship's woes continued. By late October rations were down to six ounces of bread and half a pint of water a day per man, and the men were tortured by hunger, thirst and scurvy. "Their chief consolation was to call me to see them die," Mendaña later wrote; "whenever I recall how I looked upon their death, it touches me to the soul and overcomes me."

Two more months passed with no relief from the suffering, and in December the survivors began to protest that "they no longer had any faith in charts and papers," recalled the purser, and they began muttering that the ship should turn back. Luckily for Mendaña, only another nine days now passed before they sighted land; it proved to be Baja California, and soon they were able to put into Santiago de Colima on the Mexican coast. Amazingly, the *Todos Santos* limped into the same port just a few days later. She had survived the hurricane and sailed just out of sight of the *Los Reyes* all the way back.

Ships' repairs and the tedious passage down the treacherous coast to Peru consumed nine more months. The two ships finally reached Callao on September 11, 1569. In all, they had been gone from Peru for 22½ months. They had sailed over a loop that had taken them at least 17,000 miles—and they came back with tales that were to quicken the blood of adventurers for another two centuries.

Sarmiento went on to engage in a number of imperial exploits in South America; one was a bizarre and disastrous attempt to colonize the Strait of Magellan *(page 22)*. But he played no further role in exploring the Pacific and vanished on a voyage to the East Indies in 1592.

Mendaña, however, became obsessed by thoughts of the South Pacific. Ignoring the severe trials of the voyage that had just ended, he promptly asked for a bigger and better-equipped expedition in order to exploit the islands he had found. But his uncle had been succeeded by a new Viceroy, and the incumbent Spanish bureaucrats had no enthusiasm for his discoveries. "In my opinion they were of little importance," one colonial functionary wrote to the King of Spain in 1569, "for they found no spices, nor gold and silver, nor merchandise, nor any other source of profit, and all the people were naked savages."

The official did not add—and the King needed no reminding—that

A Spanish adventurer's last, doomed dream

A decade after sailing with Alvaro de Mendaña in search of Terra Australis, Pedro Sarmiento conceived another plan to advance Spanish interests in the Pacific. He proposed that a colony be founded on the Strait of Magellan, giving Spain control of the vital passage. King Philip II agreed to back the venture—a decision he would regret.

Sarmiento sailed from Spain in September 1581 with a fleet of 23 vessels and 2,000 colonists. Within a few days, five of the ships foundered in a storm. Plagues claimed scores of victims as the fleet crossed the Atlantic, and when the ships put in at Rio de Janeiro to refit, disease and desertions took an even greater toll. Then a gale foiled Sarmiento's attempt to reach the strait in 1582. When he set out again late in 1583, the company had been reduced to five ships and 500 colonists.

The settlers—many of them, in their leader's words, "frightened and prostrate of spirit"—landed on the barren Patagonian shore in February 1584. Calling the spot Nombre de Jesús, Sarmiento started the colonists planting crops and building earthen huts.

Meanwhile, one of the ships was sent west along the coast with supplies for a second settlement. Several days later, Sarmiento set out overland with 100 soldiers to meet the supply vessel. The march took three weeks; his men, with provisions for only eight days, nearly starved. No sooner did they reach the appointed site and begin constructing the colony—called Rey Don Felipe, after their King—than the harsh Patagonian winter swept in. A two-week blizzard made it impossible even to forage for roots and shellfish.

Following his plan, Sarmiento left most of his party at Rey Don Felipe and sailed with 30 men back to Nombre de Jesús to see how the colonists there were faring. As soon as he arrived off the settlement, a gale blew his vessel out to sea—without, he recollected,

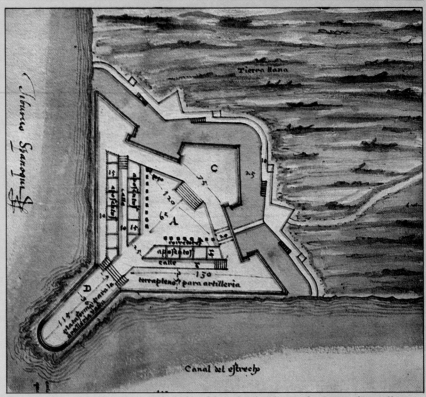

Sarmiento's unfulfilled plans included building this fort facing the Strait of Magellan.

his "even being able to take leave of friends and comrades." He sailed to Brazil and obtained new supplies, but was twice shipwrecked trying to return to Patagonia. Finally, deciding that he must ask the King for reinforcements, he headed for Spain in 1586.

Near the Azores his ship was captured by English privateers, who took him to the court of Queen Elizabeth. He discoursed with Her Majesty in Latin—"in which tongue," Sarmiento noted, "the Queen is very elegant." Charmed—and possibly intending a peaceful gesture toward Spain—she released him. But his troubles were not over. While crossing France, he was clapped into prison by a nobleman who hoped that the eminent explorer would command a great ransom.

Four years later, Sarmiento managed to buy his freedom. By now his health was broken, yet he persisted in seeking help for his settlements from

the King. His appeals went unanswered; in 1592 he accepted an appointment with a Spanish fleet bound for the East Indies, and nothing is known of him thereafter.

He could not have helped the colonists: Most of them had perished even before he made his way back to Spain. In 1587 the English privateer Thomas Cavendish had come upon the pitiful remnant of the first settlement as he passed through the strait. After three bitter winters, only 15 men and three women had survived starvation, Indian attacks and disease.

Cavendish took aboard one survivor. When the others, fearful of the English, hesitated to join him, Cavendish left them to their miserable end.

A few days later he landed at Rey Don Felipe. Finding only corpses scattered in hovels, he rechristened Sarmiento's abortive stronghold with a grimly suitable name: Port Famine.

the Spanish Empire had more urgent business at the moment than exploration. By now the other nations of Europe had scented the profits to be had in the New World and were poaching on the Spanish dominions. The French and the Dutch were founding trading posts on the fringes of the Caribbean. The English had learned that they could get rich faster through privateering, a legalized form of piracy by which the Crown discreetly supplied ships and armament to a series of daredevil adventurers—Richard Hawkins, Thomas Cavendish, Francis Drake—for a percentage of their haul. Drake's capture of one Spanish galleon in 1579 brought the stupendous harvest of 13 chests of silver coin, 26 tons of silver bullion, 80 pounds of gold and uncounted jewels. Such depredations kept Spain preoccupied during the last quarter of the 16th Century.

Throughout that period, Mendaña's obsession with the Pacific never flagged. Nor was he alone in his enthusiasm. In the waterfront taverns of Callao, mariners spun yarns about his voyage and carried them all over the world, expanding the stories in the telling. By the 1590s Mendaña's long-neglected islands seemed to be endowed with extraordinary riches: It was said that his ships had brought back 40,000 pesos of gold, that the jungle rivers flowed with more, and that the islands abounded in clove, nutmeg, ginger, pearls—and a cure for gout. As the tales traveled back across the Atlantic, the islands came to resemble the legendary Land of Ophir to which King Solomon's ships were said to have sailed in Biblical times. By association, European cartographers began to call the archipelago visited by Mendaña the Solomon Islands. Their location was vague, but to adventurers everywhere their very uncertainty had a compelling appeal. And the stories of their wealth finally helped reawaken the Spanish Crown's interest in exploration. At long last, in 1595, Mendaña won approval for another expedition.

He was now 54 years old. The long delay and the frustrations of dealing with the Spanish bureaucracy had not helped his character. He was bereft of whatever human compassion he had once shown toward his subordinates and the islanders, and he was more indecisive than ever.

He enlisted as his second-in-command and chief pilot a Portuguese navigator named Pedro Fernández de Quirós, a slim but muscular man with gray eyes and bronzed skin. Of humble origins, Quirós had gone to sea as a boy. When Portugal was united with Spain in 1580, he had automatically become a Spanish subject—and had found work piloting Spanish vessels in the New World. Now 30 years old, experienced, articulate and prudent, Quirós was competent and resourceful, but he had serious flaws that in the end would turn his life to tragedy. He was a mild-mannered man with little insight into human character. He was also a naïve dreamer and expected others to share his own religious fervor, which was excessive even in that time of evangelical exuberance.

Mendaña was given four vessels for the expedition: a square-rigged flagship named the *San Jerónimo*, another square-rigger called the *Santa Isabel*, and two large launches called the *San Felipe* and the *Santa Catalina*. Into these four ships was packed a motley assemblage of 378 prospective settlers—including a few women and children—whose mundane concerns and inexperience at sea made them hardly congenial to such an idealist as Quirós. The most troublesome of the lot was Mendaña's willful wife, an imperious and selfish aristocrat named Doña Isabel. With her came her sizable and arrogant family: three brothers with aspirations to grandeur but little talent for command, all of whom traveled with their own livestock and private stores of water, Peruvian wine and oil. Another trouble maker was the camp master, a brave but disagreeable old soldier named Pedro Merino Manrique. "He knew how to think much," said Quirós, "but he could not be silent."

Of the rest of the company, 280 were listed as "capable of bearing arms," but this did not mean they were soldiers; many were vagrants rounded up from the streets of Lima and Callao. Three priests were aboard to see to the spiritual interests of the company and to proselytize the islanders. Crowded into pens on the decks were a number of pigs intended as meat for the general company, and a pack of guard dogs.

On June 16, 1595, the vessels departed from the Peruvian coast and headed southwest for lat. 8° S., on which the Solomons were correctly calculated to lie. On reaching that latitude, Mendaña intended to sail due west about 6,000 miles—the supposed distance to the Solomons that Gallego had calculated almost three decades earlier.

Expecting a novel adventure, the company was in high spirits during the early part of the trip. Five weeks of pleasant sailing brought them in sight of land. Mendaña, fully confident that events were going according to plan, announced that the peaks stretching across the horizon were those of the Solomon Islands and ordered the *Te Deum* to be sung. But on going ashore he realized his mistake at once; the inhabitants had much lighter skin and bore no resemblance to those encountered on his previous voyage. Mendaña decided the ships would stay only long enough to water and reprovision. He named the discovery the Marquesas Islands, in honor of the Marqués de Mendoza, the current Viceroy of Lima.

The Marquesans, who proved to be friendly, had at least one behavior trait in common with the people of the Solomons; coming aboard the ships, they helped themselves to whatever they liked. But Mendaña's present company was not amused. This time, instead of chasing the interlopers off with harmless shouts of "*Afuera,*" the Spaniards fired their harquebuses, wounding several Marquesans and killing seven or eight. That was only a start; in two and a half weeks' time the soldiers killed another 200 people with equal heedlessness, drawing from Quirós the lamentation that such evil deeds "are not things to do, nor to praise, nor to allow." Mendaña seems to have offered no reproach at all.

By August 5 the Spaniards had replenished their ships' stores, and Mendaña ordered the expedition onward, assuring the company that the Solomons were right over the horizon. But days passed, then weeks, and the islands did not appear. In the darkness of a September night, one of the ships, with 180 people aboard, disappeared, never to be seen again. The soldiers and seamen on the three remaining vessels began to "murmur and talk," Quirós recorded, some saying that the ships must have passed the Solomons without anyone realizing it. And increasingly they wailed that "No one knows where we are!"

In fact, the ships had strayed more than 2° south of their intended latitude and still had not sailed far enough west. Mendaña nonetheless remained optimistic. When the ships made another landfall on Septem-

ber 7 and people paddled out in canoes, he confidently spoke to them in the tongue he recalled from his visit to the Solomons a quarter of a century before. But they did not understand a word he said.

Still, the island was large and attractive; its rising landscape reminded one of the Spaniards of the Andalusian hills of Spain. Mendaña decided after a few days of reconnoitering that it would do for a settlement and named it Santa Cruz. (The name would later be applied to the whole group of islands to which it belonged.) He thereupon ordered Merino, the camp master, and a detachment of soldiers to begin building houses at once. As the camp began to take shape, some of the colonists moved ashore, taking along the livestock and the dogs. The first European community in the South Pacific had been born.

The story of the Santa Cruz settlement is not a pleasant one. The indigenous people proved as baffling as those of the Solomons; after offering a friendly if guarded welcome, they turned surly and began shooting arrows into the ships' rigging. The Spaniards drove them off

English marauders led by Thomas Cavendish sack Puna Island off Peru and slaughter its Indian inhabitants in 1587. Cavendish was one of many English adventurers who entered the Pacific to pillage known lands rather than discover new ones. His booty from this two-year voyage came to about £125,000—nearly half the Crown's annual revenue.

with harquebuses, killing a number and wounding many more. The same kind of incident would occur again and again in the days to come.

The Spaniards also had trouble among themselves. First Mendaña and the camp master, Merino, disagreed over a site for the settlement; after vacillating, Mendaña yielded to Merino's choice. Then the soldiers detailed to do the building tired of their novel surroundings and began to grumble about how much they missed "the delights of Lima," Quirós observed ruefully. Before long the Spaniards had real cause for anguish; an unknown fever descended on the company. The first victim was Mendaña himself, who took to his bed aboard the flagship *San Jerónimo*.

Soon Doña Isabel divined that Merino was inciting the soldiers ashore to rise against Mendaña and her brothers, and she importuned her ailing husband to "kill him or have him killed." Mendaña obligingly struggled from his sickbed and, taking four trusted companions, went ashore "to do justice on the camp master," recorded Quirós. Merino came forth to meet them, and was stabbed by one of the party. "Oh gentlemen!" Merino cried out, "leave me time to confess"—and with that he fell dead. To avenge their fallen leader, Merino's men attacked Mendaña's party with swords and soon another soldier lay dead and several were wounded. Finally a shouted command from Mendaña brought the combat to a standstill, and he quickly ordered a Mass to be said, as if the invocation of the Almighty—the one authority nobody present questioned— would put an end to the matter. It did. The officiating friar delivered a sermon at the end of the Mass, urging the men to be quiet and give their obedience to Mendaña. They listened, and dispersed in peace.

By now the fever had become an epidemic and was claiming lives throughout the company every day. Two days after the brawl, Mendaña was so ill that he ordered an aide to draw up a will—which the commander was almost too weak to sign. He also summoned a friar to administer the last rites. As Mendaña prepared himself for his Maker, perhaps he found some solace in knowing that the colony he had dreamed of founding for a quarter of a century was at last a reality. By afternoon he was dead—and the colony was not to survive him for long.

According to his will, the widowed Doña Isabel became nominal governess of the expedition. The real leader, however, proved to be Quirós. He was not forceful enough to completely control the arrogant Doña Isabel but, in spite of his gentle demeanor, it was evident to all that he was better qualified to command than she was. It was to Quirós that the company began to turn for important decisions.

His first decree was to leave Santa Cruz "in the claws" of the devil. In the last month alone, 47 members of the expedition had died. Of the 280 men in the original company, only 15 were healthy; the rest were either dead or sick with the fever. Clearly the colony had no future. Quirós decided to make one last attempt to find the Solomons and then, if they missed the islands, to head for Manila, where help could be expected.

On November 18, 1595, the three ragged vessels were ready. Quirós, Doña Isabel and her family boarded the *San Jerónimo*, Mendaña's body was placed aboard the *Santa Catalina* for burial in more congenial soil, and such meager food and supplies as they could muster were dispersed among the three. In the commotion of getting under way, no one thought

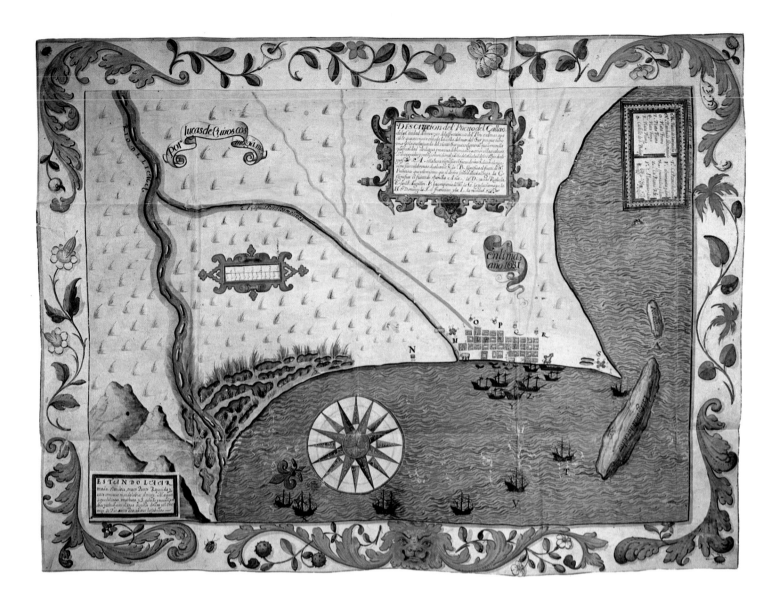

A Dutch fleet (foreground) lies at anchor off Callao, Peru, in 1624, after being seized by the Spanish during an unsuccessful Dutch attempt to take the port. Callao's location made it a logical starting point for exploration of the South Seas. Furthermore, as noted by the inscription on this commemorative map, "The cold waters, being around 12°, protect the vessels from shipworms."

of the dogs; and as the ships raised anchor and began to move, the poor creatures ran back and forth along the beach, barking at their departing masters in forlorn reproach. One of them leaped into the surf, swam for a ship and was taken on board, inspiring Quirós to reflect philosophically, "Of him it may be said that fortune favors the brave."

The same could have been said of Quirós himself. He was not quite sure where the Solomons were, and the Philippines lay more than 3,000 miles off, in seas that he had never seen and could navigate only by guess. His ships were rotten. The San Jerónimo's hull was leaking dangerously. Her mainmast was sprung from its step, her yards drooped, and some of the sails flapped uselessly for want of rope to secure them. Food supplies were so low that the daily ration for one person was limited to half a pound of flour mixed with salt water and baked in ashes—except, that is, for Doña Isabel and her brothers, whose private stores of livestock, water, Peruvian wine and oil were still ample.

Ironically, the Solomons lay less than 300 miles to the west—hardly a four-day sail in a fair wind. But Quirós steered west-southwest for two days; not seeing the islands, he turned to the northwest, narrowly missing them as he set off for the Philippines. About December 10 the ships crossed the Equator under a punishing sun. One of the smaller vessels disappeared, then the other. By New Year's Day the store of water aboard the flagship was "full of powdered cockroaches," Quirós recalled. Soon after, he sighted the island now known as Guam, and some of its inhabitants came out in canoes, offering food. The ship's company remained in dire need of fresh water, but the men were so weak that Quirós dared not risk sending them ashore to fetch some.

After nearly three months of deprivation and anguish, Quirós miraculously found the San Bernardino Strait in the Philippines, and on February 11, 1596, guided the *San Jerónimo* through the difficult shoals off Manila to a haven at last. As she approached Manila Bay, four officials in a Spanish coast guard boat came out to meet her. "They seemed like 4,000 angels," Quirós wrote. Coming aboard the *San Jerónimo*, they were astounded to see that nearly 100 men, women and babies were slowly starving to death while two of Doña Isabel's pigs frolicked about. "What the devil!" thundered one of the officials. "Is this a time for courtesy with pigs?" The petulant Doña Isabel, finding these stern men more compelling than the gentle Quirós, reluctantly yielded to their orders to have the animals killed for food immediately.

Six months later, the *San Jerónimo* had been repaired sufficiently to begin her journey back to America. No record was kept of this last and anticlimactic leg of the voyage, except that the unrepentant Doña Isabel was aboard, newly married to a well-to-do cousin of the Philippine Governor. She subsequently settled in Peru, and so far as is known never again plagued a Pacific voyage.

The Mendaña expedition had been a disaster. Of the 378 persons who had sailed from Peru in June 1595, fewer than 100 survived. The Solomons had proved elusive, and the attempted colonization of Santa Cruz had failed. For all that, Quirós had performed a remarkable feat of seamanship: He had brought a leaky vessel many thousands of miles across unknown waters, and he had brought back a reasonable estimate of the lay of the Marquesas and Santa Cruz and of the distances between them and the Philippines. So, like pieces of a mammoth jigsaw puzzle, parts of the map of the Pacific Ocean were beginning to fall into place.

Like Mendaña before him, Quirós quickly forgot the tribulations of the expedition; he was no sooner safe ashore in Peru than he took it upon himself to assume Mendaña's mission—but with a difference. He was driven by the desire to discover Terra Australis Incognita. Having found so many unexpected islands in the Pacific, he felt certain that the mythical Southern continent was there too.

In Lima he applied at once to the Viceroy for just one ship of 70 tons, along with 40 sailors, so that he could "return to discover those lands and many others that I suspect to exist, and even feel certain that I shall find, in those seas." The Viceroy referred him to the court in Spain. And now Quirós, like Mendaña before him, became engaged in a long bout with officialdom. In 1600 he crossed the Atlantic and began to petition

Spiritual pilots of the South Pacific

The Franciscan friars who sailed the Pacific with the great Spanish expeditions of the 16th Century saw their dual aim of "discovery and evangelical conquest" as a single mission: The world's lost souls had to be found before they could be saved.

Franciscans already had a long history of carrying the Gospel "to the Saracens and other infidels." Within half a century of the establishment of their order by Saint Francis of Assisi in 1210, their missionaries had traveled to Persia, Mongolia and China. And as early as 1267 a Franciscan lay brother, the Scholastic philosopher Roger Bacon, gave some advice to missionaries who found the known world too confining for their zeal: "Take the all-land route across Asia to Cathay," he wrote, "turn southwards, and at the 15° south parallel you will find the *Terra Incognita*."

But the Franciscans who voyaged in search of the unknown Southern continent—following Bacon's advice if not his directions—served more than a missionary purpose. They also gave spiritual comfort and guidance to those who sailed with them—often at critical moments. When the frightened and starving crewmen of Alvaro de Mendaña's first expedition began to fight among themselves about changing course during a hurricane, Franciscans helped stop the arguing—and thus prevented disaster—by leading the crew in religious devotions. "Thus those who were at enmity embraced each other," remembered an officer, "and we all set ourselves to help the sailors."

The explorers' sailing orders required them to consult the friars on any major decisions. But the missionaries were most influential in matters concerning the islanders, about whom many expedition members felt, as one said after some killings on Peregrina, that "it did not matter much whether the devil took them today, as he would take them in any case tomorrow."

The Franciscans strongly opposed that view, since it was their fervent wish to step between islander and devil before that tomorrow came. They counseled moderation and insisted that local people be compensated for food and water. And where the Franciscans had time to build missions—as they had in Spanish America and the Philippines—their idealism was often justified by the loyalty to Spain they engendered in their converts. "In each friar," said one official, "the King had a captain general and a whole army."

one authority after another—not only in Spain but also in Rome. Because the purpose of his mission was discovery, with the ultimate object of converting the heathen, he thought to buttress himself with scientific and ecclesiastic support. He took his case before the Spanish Ambassador to the Vatican, before Pope Clement VIII, before mathematicians and geographers, before an army of colonial bureaucrats, before the King of Spain. Back and forth he went, pleading his cause everywhere.

After a decade of dogged argument, he finally won a royal order directing the Viceroy of Peru to help him mount an expedition. Moreover, he was to have three vessels instead of one.

On December 21, 1605, Quirós' little fleet was ready to depart. The plan was to sail southwest as far as lat. 30° S., and there search for the Southern continent. If no land was sighted at 30°, the ships were to zigzag northwest and southwest until they reached Santa Cruz at 10° 20′ S. Each of the ships' captains was given sealed orders to be opened in the event that the vessels became separated.

After the long lapse since the last voyage of exploration, all Callao shared in the excitement of the departure, and people gathered on the city's rooftops to cheer the expedition on its way. Quirós' vessels were the San Pedro y Pablo, 60 tons, which he was to captain himself; the 40-ton San Pedro, under the command of Luis Váez de Torres, who was to prove indispensable to the expedition; and a launch called Los Tres Reyes Magos—small enough for coastal exploration, but strong enough to sail back to Peru with news of what the voyagers found. On board were about 300 soldiers and sailors, six Franciscan friars, provisioning for a year, and the wherewithal for founding a settlement—"iron implements, fruits and animals of Peru."

Under benign skies the ships followed the prescribed course for a full month until, on January 22, 1606, at lat. 26° S., Quirós suddenly scrapped the plan to sail all the way to 30° and shifted to a northwest tack. Why he changed course is not known; probably he was ill and his poor health was affecting his judgment. The nature of his ailment is not quite clear, but "he took such a headache from Lima," his secretary narrated, "that he could suffer neither sun nor shade." The headache, which evidently came and went, was associated with "a spasm that caused him much suffering." As the voyage progressed, Quirós seemed increasingly erratic and unable to stick to his own plans.

Sailing northwest on the new course, the ships passed several apparently uninhabited islands, then on February 10 drew close to one where a great crowd lined the beach to watch them. The presence of so many people suggested to Quirós that a large body of land must be near—Terra Australis Incognita, of course. He resolved to head southwest again, "plowing the sea with great sweeps" until he found the continent "or lost all their lives in the attempt."

His new resolve survived no longer than his last one. Quirós' chief pilot, Juan Ochoa de Bilboa, promptly challenged the orders, and the commander, "finding himself very ill and overwhelmed by cares of many kinds," changed his mind. It might indeed be best, he concluded, to steer along lat. 10° 20′ for Santa Cruz, build a new encampment and "begin to make discoveries from there, as if we were starting from Lima."

On March 1 they neared another inhabited island, and people came out in canoes, "singing to the sound of their paddles," one Spaniard later recalled. Naming the island Peregrina (it was probably Rakahanga in the northern Cook Islands), Quirós stopped for water and wood.

The Spaniards had no sooner landed than they disobeyed orders to behave humanely. One soldier seized four islanders and tried to ransom them for food; having no luck, he tried to force his way into a hut. The resident, holding his ground, struck the soldier with a club, whereupon another soldier shot the man and then finished him off with a sword. Many other killings followed before the Spaniards left the island.

They departed without enough water to carry them far, and as the men grew restive with thirst and boredom, they began to blame Quirós for their ills. They grumbled that he had deceived both the Pope and the King and that he was leading them all nowhere. Alarmed, Quirós placed a block for a hangman's rope at the yardarm as a warning that anyone guilty of further subversive talk would be executed. In that dark mood of mutual ill feeling, the travelers proceeded for two more weeks.

Then at last they began to sight birds, sea snakes and drifting wood. On April 7 a boy perched at the masthead of the flagship cried out, "Land to the northwest, high and black." No one was more relieved than Quirós, who expected to find that they had arrived at Santa Cruz. Coming closer, he saw that they had not. Nor was this island one of the Solomons; he had made an error in figuring his latitude and was a few minutes north of his intended landfall at 10° 20′ S.

There was nothing to do but make the best of it. Quirós went ashore and befriended a handsome, gray-bearded chief named Tumai and learned the island was called Taumako (it has retained the name in modern times, and is a member of the Duff Group). Because the people here were seafarers and sailed far and wide in outrigger canoes, Tumai was able to give an impressive account of South Sea geography. By sign language, he told Quirós of many lands, indicating which were small and which were large, explaining which peoples were light-skinned and which were dark, which were friendly and which were not—conveying, by biting his arm, that some were cannibals. To show distances, he pointed to the sun, then rested his head on his hand, shut his eyes and with his fingers counted the number of nights' sleep a voyage took. When he described many islands to the south as being larger and lusher than Santa Cruz, Quirós abruptly changed his mind again and decided to head in that direction. The ships left Taumako at sunset on April 18.

Tumai's information proved correct. As they moved on, they saw islands everywhere; in three days' time the Spaniards counted eight, all of them lush and beautiful. On April 29 a large body of land rose up on the southwest horizon. The nearer they drew, the better it looked; one of the officers, recalling the vision, described it as "a great land with high mountains, which promised to be no less than continental." The island was one of a 400-mile-long group now known as the New Hebrides. The largest of the islands is more than 70 miles long, and they are so arranged in overlapping tiers that from afar they appear to be a single land mass. On May 3 the ships dropped anchor in a broad, deep bay (later known as the Bay of St. Philip and St. James). The whole company was elated, and when someone pronounced the place "the most abundant and powerful land ever discovered by Spaniards," no one disagreed.

Going ashore, Quirós was overjoyed with what he found. Rolling open land led to a green and mountainous interior, and the climate was perfect. "I can say with good reason," he later wrote, "that a land more delightful, healthy and fertile, a site better supplied with quarries, timber, clay for tiles, bricks for founding a great city on the sea, with a port and a river on a plain, with level terrain near the hills, or better adapted to raise plants and all that Europe and the Indies produce, could not be found."

Feeling like a pilgrim come at last to the promised land, he decided to call his new city New Jerusalem, and the river that coursed through the site would be the Jordan. To the land itself he gave a compound name that reflected his love of symbolism; it would be Austrialia del Espíritu Santo, a play on words meaning "Austria of the Holy Spirit." It evoked images of the long-sought Terra Australis Incognita and simultaneously honored both Philip III—now King of Spain and also Archduke of Austria—and the Holy Ghost, the divine spirit that Quirós believed had led him there. He was in ecstasy.

Meaning to lose no time in getting his settlement under way, Quirós sent Luis Váez de Torres, the *San Pedro's* commander, ashore with a detachment of soldiers to reconnoiter the country and capture some inhabitants, so that the friars could convert them to Christianity and thus demonstrate "the good work we intended for them."

This assignment proved less easy than he had expected, for these were not friendly folk like those on Tumai's island, but a congregation of warring tribes who would brook no incursions into their territory. Torres and his group had no sooner stepped onto the beach than they were halted by a large number of warriors. Their chief drew a line in the sand, making clear that the Spaniards were not to cross it; by signs, he indicated that his people would lay down their arms if the Spaniards would do likewise and honor the line of demarcation. Before Torres could respond to the proposition, an underling lost his head and fired, killing one warrior and scattering the rest. To cow other inhabitants, the Spaniards hung the dead man's body from a tree. Just then, another chief advanced from the woods, "making a sound on a shell with great force." The Spaniards shot him instantly.

Disappointed but undeterred on hearing of the violence, Quirós proceeded with the business of settling in. On May 13 he established a ministry of war and marine, appointing Torres as camp master and charging 18 other ministers with the safety of the colony. He followed this up by proclaiming a new chivalric order, calling it the Knights of the Holy Ghost and admitting to membership all those on the expedition. The new knights were given blue taffeta crosses to wear on their chests as badges of the order.

The climax to Quirós' pageantry came with the feast of Pentecost. On the eve of the holy day the ships were illuminated with oil lanterns. Rockets and fire wheels soared into the night sky, and the ships' boys dressed in colored silks, wore bells on their feet and performed a sword dance for the amusement of their elders. Early the next morning Torres and a group of his ministers went ashore and constructed the colony's

estaxente es desta baia s felipe y s tiago Donde senos fuela cӡpitana sonnegrosde
cuerpos horͻ dinarios sus armas son flechas Daͻ dos ymaͻanas ӡ hͻeͻͻaforͻhL
ysana tapanlasber euencas con ofas ͻeaͻboles ⁓

first building out of palm boughs. Part church and part fort, it had an altar at one end and four small cannon at the other. Quirós, officiating at the dedication of this hybrid edifice, was rhapsodic. "O Land!" he cried, "sought for so long, intended to be found by many, and so desired by me." The friars celebrated Mass, and the guns thundered in salute. The ceremonies over, "we went to dine under the shade of great tufted trees near a clear running stream," Quirós noted in his journal, ending the day with a perfect sense of well-being.

As time passed, his knights found themselves less formal entertainment: They roamed about the countryside, routed inhabitants from ceremonial dances, raided huts and helped themselves to livestock. One day they came back to the ship with 12 pigs and eight chickens; on another, their haul included three young boys. Quirós was so delighted with the boys—the first potential converts for his missionary efforts—that he was unmoved by their pleading to be returned to their families. "Silence, child," he admonished one of them. "You know not what you ask. Greater good awaits you than the sight and communion of heathen parents."

Just when it seemed that all was going as he wished, Quirós suddenly—and with no warning—altered all his plans. On May 25 he marched inland about three miles and returned to the ship with a stunning announcement. The expedition would leave Espíritu Santo next day and visit the lands to the south. Except for a vague reference to native hostil-

In this watercolor by a member of Pedro Fernández de Quirós' 1605-1606 expedition, New Hebrides islanders show off their primitive weapons, including clubs with curved heads. Besides fashioning weapons from coconut palms like those at left, the islanders ate the coconuts, made sails from the leaves and built houses of the wood.

esta xente es del rremate dela nueva guinea esenuebez mexa ·sus armas son dardos escudos largos flechas lanças largas montantes decat ß cegai los contrarios aqui vsande sienno ding poco y al ounas cositas de Ghina porq eluema tz della tierra escuspeama de golei q delacpiomeilul maliae

Although he painted them with black skins, the artist's inscription says these New Guineans were of "a reddish-colored" race. This watercolor and the one opposite are from a group of four by the same anonymous Spaniard; they are thought to be the only existing contemporary pictures from the whole era of Spanish exploration in the Pacific.

ity, the unpredictable Quirós gave no clue to his reason for abruptly choosing to turn his back on the most promising land yet discovered in the South Seas—and after only three weeks' trial.

He now embarked on a whole new round of mishaps. The day the ships left the harbor, a stiff southeast wind blew them to the north. Aboard the *San Pedro y Pablo*, Quirós suddenly changed his mind once again and contravened his earlier order; signaling the other two ships, he announced that the company would return to Espíritu Santo and spend the winter. But the same contrary wind also made it difficult to regain the anchorage. The *San Pedro*, under the command of Torres, made it, and so did the launch. Quirós could not, and as darkness closed in, a severe squall came up and blew the *San Pedro y Pablo* out of the bay.

Next morning those aboard the *San Pedro y Pablo* found that they were many miles out to sea. For three days they attempted to regain the bay, to no avail. Finally, Quirós perversely decided to resume his plan to sail for Santa Cruz—hoping that Torres would join him there, although he had no means of telling him to do so. He ordered a course due north for Santa Cruz's latitude of 10° 20′. Then, once he was at the desired latitude, Quirós could not decide whether to sail east or west to find the island. In the face of his indecision, the rest of the ship's company held a conference and decided to return to America.

One of the officers on Torres' ship wrote later that he thought a mutiny must have taken place on Quirós' vessel, and that the mutineers must have forced the commander to sail home. But there is no evidence of mutiny. It simply appears that Quirós had lost control over events—and with it his last chance to capitalize on his discovery of Espíritu Santo.

Nothing but disappointments remained for him. He reached Acapulco on November 23, 1606, and—incredibly—at once set off for Madrid to beg for another expedition. He was there for the better part of a decade, writing, arguing, petitioning the King, publishing 50 memorials and drawing 200 maps—only to be repulsed at every turn. Clearly, Quirós lacked judgment in a venture where judgment was vital, and the Spanish Crown wanted no more of him. Returning to South America, he died in Panama in 1615, at the age of 50, without any prospect of bringing off his hoped-for expedition. No record survives of his final ailment, but exhaustion and mental anguish had undoubtedly worn him down.

When Quirós left Torres behind in the bay at Espíritu Santo, the chief pilot searched everywhere in the nearby waters for his commander's ship. He also climbed the headlands of Espíritu Santo to scan the horizon in all directions, but saw no sign of Quirós' vessel. After waiting two weeks, he opened the sealed orders he had been given for just such an eventuality and assumed command himself.

And effective command it was. The orders directed him to sail the remaining two ships to 20° S. in search of Terra Australis Incognita, then northwest to 4° and thence past New Guinea to Manila. A number of the officers, weary now of adventure, objected to the prospect of voyaging farther into unknown waters, and clamored to return home. But Torres was determined to obey his instructions—and the ships' company yielded and did as he bade them.

Commanding the launch to follow along, he first sailed to the end of Espíritu Santo, satisfying himself that it was an island and not a continent, as they had first thought it to be. He then headed southwest to 20°, as directed, and for good measure continued on to 21°. Seeing no land, he followed the next step, which was to steer northwest for New Guinea. Reaching its southeast corner (and recognizing it, presumably, from traders' accounts), he tried to sail along the known northern coast until he could clear it for the Philippines. But the winds were against him, "so I coasted along to the westward on the south side." Thus, with tantalizing brevity, Torres describes an epochal move in Pacific exploration. He was the first European explorer to see the southern limits of that major Pacific island—and thus to prove that it was indeed an island, not a projection of Terra Australis Incognita, as many geographers believed.

The coast along which the two vessels now groped was full of shoals, and the going was slow. There were many harbors, and Torres visited several of them. Everywhere, he was accosted by hostile New Guineans—naked except for bark cloth around their waists, and armed with darts, shields and clubs decorated with feathers. The Spaniards could see smoke signals in the hilltops by day and fires by night, as if the inhabitants were conveying to one another news of the ships' passage.

After several weeks of sailing westward along this coast, the visitors found themselves threading their way through innumerable small is-

A tracery of voyages across the trackless ocean

The three Spanish expeditions into the Pacific between 1567 and 1606 traveled west through uncharted waters as far as the Solomons and the New Hebrides— traversing about a third of the earth's circumference. In 1596 Quirós returned by way of the Philippines. In 1606 he went home by way of Mexico, while Torres went on separately to the Philippines.

lands. The currents were so strong that two men were needed at the helm, yet the water was so shallow that they could sometimes feel the ship scraping the bottom. Finally, in the third week of October, almost four months after leaving Espíritu Santo, they reached the western end of New Guinea, almost 1,500 miles from their first landfall.

Torres had sailed through the hitherto undiscovered and extremely difficult strait between New Guinea and the then-unknown land of Australia. Whether or not he actually sighted Australia, whose location and size make it the closest approximation in real geography to the fabled Terra Australis Incognita, is not recorded. Seven months later, after a passage through the Moluccas, he reached Manila. There he submitted a report on his voyage, but the Spaniards hid it away; they did not wish to publicize to the English and Dutch the existence of new paths. Not for another 150 years would it be known that Torres had been through the strait; in 1762 the British seized Manila from the Spaniards and, finding Torres' report, affixed his name to the strait.

And long before then, the age of Spanish exploration in the Pacific had ended. That endeavor, beginning with Magellan's circumnavigation early in the 16th Century, had been capped by the work of two navigators who led Spanish ships to the farthest known reaches of the great ocean. Neither Quirós nor Torres had found Terra Australis Incognita. But they had broadened European knowledge in reporting the existence of hundreds of islands, with strange inhabitants and exotic ways of life.

Meanwhile, another people had taken up the quest: the Spaniards' former subjects in the newly independent Netherlands.

The Dutchman who cracked the Spanish dominion

Olivier van Noort, the Dutch privateer who defied Spain in the Pacific, shares this 17th Century engraving with two earlier circumnavigators.

The Dutch took up Pacific exploration almost by accident. During most of the 16th Century, while the Spaniards mined the riches of the Americas and their Portuguese subjects monopolized the spice routes around the Cape of Good Hope, Holland's stolid Calvinist burghers—the pre-eminent maritime merchants of their day—were content to make a steady income by carrying goods from Spanish entrepôts to other European ports.

A miscalculation by Philip II of Spain disrupted this comfortable state of affairs. Claiming sovereignty over the Dutch, in 1594 he tried to coerce them into submission by closing Spain's ports to their shipping. The embargo backfired dramatically. These superb seafarers, denied the rich spice trade from Lisbon and Cádiz, began dispatching their own expeditions to the East Indies. The most ambitious of their voyages was led by a Rotterdam innkeeper and former privateer named Olivier van Noort, who became the first Dutchman to circle the globe—and in the process clearly signaled the end of Spanish hegemony in the Pacific.

Although ostensibly embarking on an ordinary spice-trading venture, van Noort planned from the outset to prey on the Spanish and their treasure ships. In a petition to the Dutch government, he proposed to sail by way of the Spanish possessions along the west coast of America—curious ports of call for a spice trader—and requested cannon, gunpowder and a commission as an admiral in the Dutch Navy.

The government agreed and van Noort, with 200,000 guilders raised by private subscription, bought and outfitted two vessels for the voyage—the 275-ton *Mauritius*, a superbly seaworthy ship about 130 feet long, and the 50-ton *Eendracht*, a fast, fine-lined vessel of the kind the Dutch called a yacht. Two ships from Amsterdam, the 350-ton *Hendrick Frederick* and the 50-ton yacht *Hope*, also sailed under Admiral van Noort's command. The expedition had no sooner set out in 1598 than it ran into trouble. In the Gulf of Guinea off the African coast, Portuguese soldiers at Príncipe Island promised to help the Dutch get fresh water, then massacred the landing party. On the other side of the Atlantic some weeks later, Portuguese soldiers ambushed van Noort at Rio de Janeiro and incited Indians to bushwhack the Dutch wherever they landed.

The Southern Hemisphere's winter was approaching as van Noort neared the stormy Strait of Magellan in March 1599, so he retreated to Brazil's desolate Santa Clara Island to await spring. There his wretched, scurvy-stricken company found fresh fruit, overhauled three of their ships and burned the *Eendracht*, which was leaky beyond repair, giving her name to the *Hope*.

When the Dutch at last entered the strait, they had to battle a westerly gale. They took 116 days to fight their way through the treacherous passage and past fierce Indians; by the time they reached the Pacific, 100 of the original 248

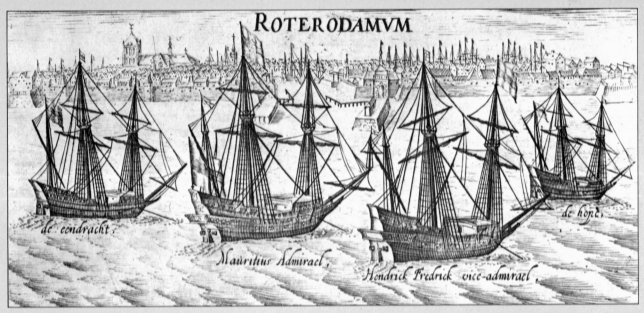

Van Noort's fleet awaits departure from Rotterdam in this fanciful engraving. The ships actually sailed from the province of Zeeland.

Van Noort and his men swarm ashore to avenge the murder of their comrades by Portuguese soldiers on Príncipe Island, off the African coast. This engraving, compressing a sequence of events, shows the Dutch assaulting the fort (upper right), refilling their water casks (center) and attacking a village (left). They were repulsed by the fort's defenders, but burned the island's sugar plantations.

Set afire because her hull was too rotten to repair, the first Eendracht burns while sailors seine for fish and hunt birds on Santa Clara Island off Brazil. Her name—Dutch for "concord"—was given to the Hope, the vessel just behind the burning ship, when the captain of that yacht died and was replaced by the captain of the scuttled Eendracht.

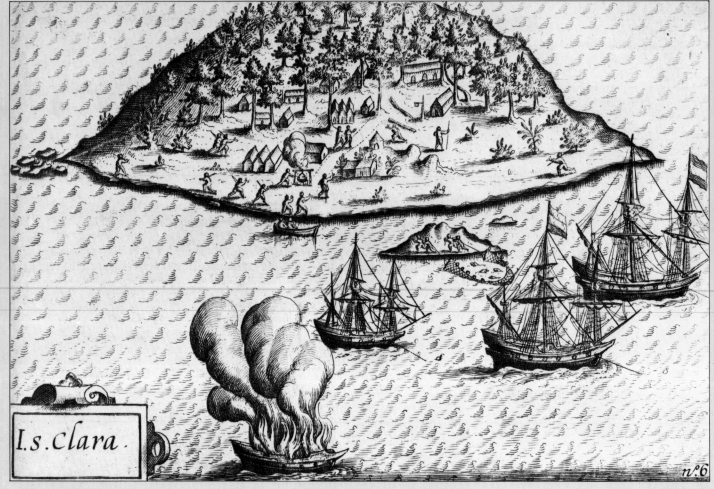

men had died from disease or wounds. Less than a month later the *Hendrick Frederick* disappeared in a storm. (She eventually crossed the Pacific alone and was sold to a Moluccan sultan, her crew returning home in a Dutch ship.)

Left with only two ships and 90 men, van Noort nevertheless pressed north to raid Spanish shipping along the South American coast. He was foiled at every turn. The vigilant Spanish Navy constantly pursued the tiny fleet, and no treasure ships materialized. In mid-May, 1600, after three trying months, van Noort sailed west along the Equator toward Spain's Philippine colonies.

He thoroughly terrorized the poorly defended Philippines, but again the coveted Spanish bullion eluded him. When in desperation he brazenly waited at the mouth of Manila harbor for an incoming treasure fleet, two galleons

Patagonian warriors attack a landing party in the Strait of Magellan, spraying the Dutch with arrows and even pelting them from the cliffs with penguins. The Dutch musketeers annihilated the men of the tribe while the women and children cowered in a nearby cave, then kidnapped half a dozen children to exhibit as curiosities in Holland.

S. Maria.

Seeking Spanish gold, the Mauritius (left) and the Eendracht pursue the galleon Buen Jesus near the Chilean island of Santa María. The speedy Dutch privateers quickly overhauled the Spaniard—and discovered that they had captured a worthless cargo of lard and corn meal. Only later did they learn that the Spanish captain had thrown 10,200 pounds of gold overboard during the chase.

In the Marianas, islanders in sailing canoes throng around the Dutch ships, bartering fresh food for scraps of ironwork. These incorrigible swindlers often sold rice mixed with stones and filled the bottoms of their food baskets with coconut shells—the same behavior that, 80 years earlier, had prompted Magellan to name the Marianas the Islands of the Thieves.

Isle de Ladrones

Bapt. a Doet. fec.

captured the yacht and routed van Noort in the *Mauritius*. He then set sail for Borneo, but even in the fabulous Spice Islands he failed to find a rich cargo. With only 44 demoralized men left, he sailed for home via the Cape of Good Hope.

Van Noort received a chilly reception from his shareholders when the *Mauritius*, her hold nearly empty, docked at Rotterdam on August 26, 1601. He had failed as a privateer and as a merchant—and also as an explorer, having crossed the vast Pacific without discovering any new lands.

But his travels were not entirely fruitless. Within a month of his arrival he published a journal of the voyage. Widely reprinted, it proved that Spain and Portugal no longer controlled the Pacific, and helped lure a new generation of Dutchmen, whose experiences would be both more prosaic and more profitable than van Noort's, into those waters.

A 300-ton Spanish galleon (center) opens fire on the Mauritius (right) outside Manila harbor, while a second galleon blasts the tiny Eendracht behind a Chinese pilot junk (left) that the Dutch had commandeered. The Eendracht was taken, but though boarders overwhelmed the Mauritius, van Noort's threat to blow up her powder magazine scared them off.

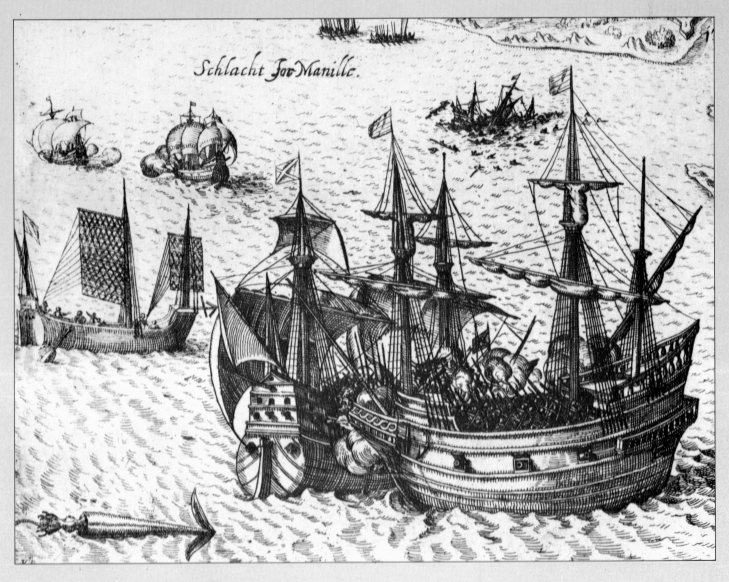

Schlacht for Manille.

Chapter 2

Searching for business in a watery wilderness

The Dutch merchantman Eendracht, the first ship to reach the Pacific via the Strait of Le Maire, returns to a port near Rotterdam in 1618.

n October 28, 1615, Captain Willem Corneliszoon Schouten assembled his crew on the deck of the 220-ton *Eendracht,* a stout, round-hulled Dutch ship riding the Atlantic swells somewhere off the coast of South America. Nearby, men on the 110-ton *Hoorn,* the *Eendracht's* sister ship, waited eagerly to get a report on what Schouten was about to tell their companions. Almost five months had passed since the two vessels had left Holland, and in all that time the crews had never been told where they were heading. They knew only that they had been signed on by a mysterious group called the Australian Company. Around the docks at home their ships had acquired a promising nickname: the gold seekers. But where was the gold? Why was everything so secret?

The reason was soon apparent: Schouten announced to his assembled crew that they were on a clandestine voyage of discovery to the Pacific. He and Jacob Le Maire, a young Dutchman who shared command of the expedition with him, had waited to explain their mission until they were far from any port where their men might leak the news. They were operating outside the authority and in virtual defiance of the Dutch East India Company, the commercial agency that monopolized Holland's trade with the Indies.

That company's charter gave it control of all Dutch shipping through the Strait of Magellan. Therefore the *Eendracht* (the second Dutch Pacific voyager to bear that name) and the *Hoorn* could reach the South Seas only if Schouten and Le Maire discovered a new route around the bottom of South America. Schouten, a veteran navigator, was not at all sure such a passage existed. But he said that if the expedition did find a way into the Pacific, they might "discover new countries where, according to some, great wealth can be got."

Schouten's words brought cheers from the men on the *Eendracht.* Then it was Le Maire's turn to speak. He had with him a Dutch translation of a memorial that Pedro Fernández de Quirós had written to the Spanish court five years earlier to win royal backing for further exploration, and he now read aloud some of Quirós' passages describing Terra Australis Incognita.

In the South Seas somewhere west of Peru, claimed the Spaniard, lay a great land, "an earthly paradise. The population is numerous. It is a decent people, clean, cheerful and reasonable. The fruits are numerous and good. There are bananas of six kinds, a great number of almonds, many earth nuts, oranges and lemons. The riches are silver and pearls, which I saw, and gold." On hearing this, some of the men wrote the magic name Terra Australis inside their caps with chalk so they could commit it to memory later.

Despite the ringing certainty of Quirós' description, the Southern continent was as much a mystery in 1615 as it had been when the Spaniards began their explorations in the mid-16th Century. Prevailing opinion still held that a large land mass lay somewhere between New Guinea and the southern end of South America. The discovery of the Solomon Islands, Santa Cruz and Espíritu Santo had filled in only a corner of the blank space stretching across the maps of the Southern Hemisphere. The Dutch were to clarify the picture dramatically.

The 17 directors of the Dutch East India Company—the trading monopoly that financed virtually all of their country's Pacific exploration—convene in their Amsterdam headquarters in 1602. "With God's aid," said one of the company officials, "we may obtain some great booty in the South Seas."

They were well suited to the task. Holland, poor in land, had long been a country of seafarers, possessing both a flourishing fishing industry and a lucrative maritime trade that reached across the world. "Remember we are all sailors," declared one Dutch captain of the era, "accustomed from our cradle to the ocean, while yonder Spaniards are mainly soldiers and landsmen, qualmish at the smell of bilge water, and sickening at the roll of the waves."

The Dutch were not interested in converting souls, plundering for gold or subjugating island populations; they simply wished to make money through commerce. As a result, they produced a new kind of explorer, sober and efficient rather than daring or inspired. Many of their discoveries were only dutifully recorded chance encounters during routine commercial voyages; others were the result of business-like expeditions in search of better routes or new markets. But their dogged, expert captains were the right men for the methodical job of mapping the uncharted coasts they would encounter.

The Dutch East India Company, founded in 1602, was the chief instrument of the country's maritime power. It was as much an agency of war and diplomacy as of commerce. Company representatives operating out of Eastern headquarters in what was then called Jacatra, Java, were empowered to make treaties with foreign princes and to build forts and maintain armed forces. They rapidly acquired major trading concessions from local rulers and gradually gained control of the routes leading to and from the Pacific. In the process they virtually eliminated the English and Portuguese as significant rivals for commerce in the Eastern seas. The Spanish still held the Philippines, but their trade was modest compared with the activities of the Dutch.

In its early years the company showed little interest in exploration for its own sake. But Dutchmen outside the company were intrigued by the rumors of an undiscovered continent. In 1610 Isaac Le Maire, a wealthy Amsterdam merchant and outspoken critic of the company's jealous dominance of Far Eastern trade, founded the rival Australian Company. He wrested permission from the government to "go trade in the kingdoms of Tatary, China, Japan, India, Terra Australis." He did not, however, receive permission to use the company-controlled passages around the Cape of Good Hope or through the Strait of Magellan—and thus had no choice but to establish a new route.

Earlier explorers had speculated that Tierra del Fuego, the land south of the strait, was part of an archipelago through which there might be several alternate passages. But the cold, gale-swept region was believed to be so hazardous to navigation that no one had yet ventured to explore it. Isaac Le Maire, with the riches of the Orient and the legendary Southern continent to lure him on, considered the navigational risks well worth running. He entrusted the job to his 29-year-old son Jacob and to Willem Schouten, who had made three previous voyages to the Indies.

After the joint commanders had divulged the nature of their mission on that October day, they continued to the south and in due course reached the coast of Patagonia. There, when the two ships were beached and careened for cleaning, the *Hoorn* caught fire and was destroyed. The entire company of 89 men piled aboard the *Eendracht*, crept past the entrance to the Strait of Magellan and headed into the waters to the south. For five days they skirted the island of Tierra del Fuego. On January 25 they spied a mass of land to the southeast, which Schouten described as "very high and perilous, extending on the north side to the east-southeast, as far as we could see."

The explorers baptized it Staten Land after the States-General, Holland's legislative body, and headed into the broad strait—subsequently honored with Jacob Le Maire's surname—that separated it from Tierra del Fuego. A day and a half later they emerged into the open sea, and on January 29 they rounded a gaunt headland that appeared to be the southern tip of Tierra del Fuego (it is, in fact, the tip of another island, 65 miles farther south). They decided to name the headland after their home port of Hoorn. The world would later come to know it by an anglicized version of the name: Cape Horn.

Schouten and Le Maire were well aware that their discovery of an open-sea alternative to the labyrinthian Strait of Magellan was momentous. But the Dutchmen were more excited by Staten Land. Schouten and Le Maire speculated that it was the eastern tip of the promised Southern continent.

After such tingling developments, the rest of the voyage was a letdown. The explorers expected to find more of the continent to their west. But they saw no other signs of the fabled land mass—nor anything else much resembling an earthly paradise. After rounding the Horn, the *Eendracht* was forced northward by potent westerlies. The long swells marching in from the west indicated to the experienced Schouten that no large land could be very near.

Off the coast of Chile heavy storms tossed the Dutchmen aimlessly about for more than a month before they picked up the southeasterly trades and sped west. In early April they reached the Tuamotu Islands, where they took on water, medicinal herbs, some "snails of very good flavor" and a plague of flies that continued to swarm over the hapless little ship for three days after it had fled hastily into open waters. In early April they sailed through the Tongas, becoming the first Europeans to see those Polynesian islands. Heading northwest, they arrived at a small island group that, in another display of home-port loyalty, they named the Hoorn Islands. The inhabitants, after some initial displays of hostility, welcomed the Dutch with crowns of feathers and feasts of roast pigs, accompanied by music and dancing. They "showed us much honor and amity," wrote Le Maire.

The young Dutchman thought that these pleasant islands matched the description Quirós had given of lands the Spaniard believed were just east of Terra Australis. He was sure that the expedition had arrived in the Solomons and that not far to the west lay the fabulous continent. But Schouten placed more weight on the expedition's shortage of supplies than on the possibility of finding the promised land. To Le Maire's disappointment, he insisted on abandoning the search and heading for Java. The *Eendracht* set sail for the northwest on June 1, followed the known route around the northern coast of New Guinea, and arrived at Jacatra in October 1616.

New gateway to the Pacific

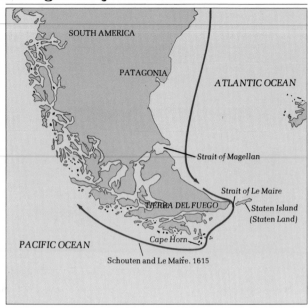

Willem Schouten and Jacob Le Maire were the first European navigators to round South America by a route other than the Strait of Magellan. Because the strait was controlled by a rival Dutch trading company, they continued south past its Atlantic entrance and found a passage to the west between Tierra del Fuego and another island, which they called Staten Land. They named the newfound waterway the Strait of Le Maire.

There the explorers were met by the local Governor General of the East India Company, who refused to believe they could have come around South America by any route other than the Strait of Magellan. As punishment for their alleged flouting of a company regulation, he confiscated the *Eendracht* and sent Schouten and Le Maire back to Holland (the ship was returned there two years later). Jacob Le Maire died on the way home, at the age of 31. Henceforth any exploring by the Dutch would have to be done on company time.

The first official Dutch East India Company probe of the Pacific had been sent out a decade before the voyage of Schouten and Le Maire. It was a relatively modest effort, aimed at the southern coast of New Guinea. The island's northern coast had been charted nearly a hundred years earlier by the Spanish, who had dubbed it the "land of gold"—in hope, rather than with cause—and had theorized that it might be the northernmost edge of the great Southern continent. The company leaders in Java thought it would be worthwhile to investigate this "land called Nova Guinea, which, it is said, is rich in gold," and in 1605 they dispatched a pinnace called the *Duyfken*. The little ship ran down the western side of New Guinea and followed the southern coast to the east for some 880 miles. Then, coming upon shoal-filled waters, the Dutchmen turned south, apparently thinking that the shallows indicated the entrance to a bay and that there was no opening to the east. Thus they sailed right across the western mouth of the strait that the Spanish explorer Luis Váez de Torres was to discover only five months later.

Their new course brought them to the barren western shore of what is now known as Australia's Cape York Peninsula. Without realizing it—still thinking they were somewhere off New Guinea—they had indeed discovered a new continent. They probably would have been disappointed had they known this, for the land was nothing like the glittering dominion of legend. Not only was the terrain desolate, but the inhabitants were wild and cruel. "In sending their men on shore to intreat of trade, there were nine of them killed by the heathens, who are maneaters," reported a crew member a year later. "So they were constrained to return, finding no good to be done there."

The unprepossessing results of the *Duyfken* expedition dampened what little ardor the company had for adventuring. For the next four decades most of its discoveries in the South Seas would be the incidental by-products of commercial voyages. The most significant of these came after the Dutch discovered a new eastward route to the Indies.

Ever since the earliest days of the Indies trade, the preferred path had been by way of the Cape of Good Hope rather than through the Strait of Magellan, where the prevailing westerlies made progress difficult. Following the route pioneered by the Portuguese, Dutch mariners rounded Africa, hugged the continent's eastern coast as far as the Arabian Sea, crossed over to India and sailed southeast from there to Java. In 1611 they learned that by running 4,000 miles due east from the Cape before the prevailing westerlies, then turning and sailing directly north, they could cut their travel time by more than half. By 1615 almost all of the company's ships were following the new route and getting from Holland to

Hoornſe Eijlandt
Iſle de Hoorn

Hostile inhabitants of the Hoorn Islands try to repulse a landing party (lower left) from Jacob Le Maire's Eendracht on April 30, 1616. Following this brief skirmish, amity prevailed, and the local chieftain invited the Dutch voyagers back to his hut for a sumptuous repast (inset) of roast pig and fruit. "We got to be as free and easy," wrote Le Maire, "as if we had been at home."

Jacatra in a breathtaking six to eight months. Inevitably, given the difficulties in determining longitude at that time, some of the ships sailed too far to the east before turning north, and they began running into a large body of land far to the south of Java.

In 1616 a vessel commanded by Captain Dirk Hartog bumped into a sandy island off what seemed to be a mainland coast around lat. 26° S. Hartog disembarked, briefly inspected the place and nailed a pewter dish to a post to record his visit. He then climbed back aboard and sailed on, having unwittingly discovered the westernmost part of Australia.

Three years later Frederick de Houtman, in command of two ships bound for Java, happened on a shore about 150 miles south of Hartog's island. The coast appeared to be of red mud—a typical gold-bearing soil—and Houtman concluded that this must be a fabulous land that had been described centuries earlier by the Venetian explorer Marco Polo. In the course of his Eastern travels, Polo had been told of a country named Beach, which was said to abound in elephants, rare spices and gold. Polo was actually describing Cambodia and the Malay Peninsula, but many Europeans interpreted his account as evidence of a rich Southern island. Accordingly, Houtman in his journal called his own discovery "this south-land of Beach." Heavy surf prevented his landing, however, and he sailed on, "being content with having seen the land, which at more favorable time may be more fully explored with more fitting vessels and smaller craft."

But the company did not immediately pursue Houtman's find. Although Dutch captains continued to sight bits and pieces of this mysterious land, and kept an eye out for it as a navigational aid, they were more interested in getting their ships into port than in stopping to investigate largely uninviting shores. Still, their accumulated findings obviously amounted to something substantial. Since most of the reports indicated that it was unlike either Marco Polo's Beach or Terra Australis Incognita, the company leaders invented a new and unmistakably proprietary name for the land: New Holland.

The company's Eastern operations were now under the authority of Governor General Jan Coen, an energetic leader who had expanded the Jacatra headquarters and renamed the town Batavia, the Roman name for Holland. In 1622, Coen drew up a comprehensive plan to explore New Holland's coastline, investigate its resources and determine if it was connected to the still-puzzling southern portion of New Guinea. Even if the explorers discovered nothing of value, they would perform a useful service by charting the New Holland coast, whose hidden shoals were a threat to Dutch ships and their costly cargoes. Coen's ambitious scheme was never carried out. The two vessels he earmarked for the expedition were needed for more prosaic duties, and several months later he was recalled to Holland.

The following year, however, two other ships, the *Arnhem* and the *Pera*, were sent out on a scaled-down expedition to further explore southern New Guinea. The results were not encouraging. The ships followed the route the *Duyfken* had taken 18 years earlier. The captain of the *Arnhem* and nine of his men were killed in a fight with New Guineans, and the remainder of the company missed the Torres Strait and

crossed to Cape York Peninsula. There they became separated when the men of the *Arnhem* rebelliously struck out to the west on their own; Captain Jan Carstenz of the *Pera* later charged that they were seeking an inhabited island "to have a good time of it"—presumably with the female inhabitants. But the *Arnhem's* crew found no fun, only a previously undiscovered stretch of Australia's northern coast, which they named Arnhem Land. They then returned to Java, arriving three weeks before the *Pera*, which had gone home by retracing her route along New Guinea's southern coast.

Captain Carstenz delivered a glum report on the expedition. The land to the south of New Guinea, he wrote, "is very dry and barren. We have not seen one fruit-bearing tree, nor anything that man can make use of. In our judgment this is the most arid and barren region that could be found anywhere on earth." Company officials in Java considered the expedition a miserable failure. "They have done nothing worth mentioning," one wrote irritably.

Meanwhile, ships coming from the northern country continued to blunder into the western coast of this land. In 1627 a ship called the *Gulden Zeepaert*, outbound from the Netherlands under skipper François Thijssen, wandered so far off course that she came upon the southern edge of New Holland. Thijssen, displaying more curiosity than most of his colleagues, followed the coastline east for fully 1,000 miles. At

Officials supervise the delivery of trade goods in Batavia, the Javan port where the Dutch East India Company built an imposing compound (background) as its Far East headquarters. Batavia was ideally situated for exploiting the riches of Indonesia, but it was steamy and low-lying, and so disease-ridden that one visitor called it "the land of death."

length he came across two small groups of islands, which he named St. Francis and St. Peter after the namesake saints of himself and a passenger, Pieter Nuyts, an East India Company official. At that point Thijssen decided that he had wasted enough time. He came about and headed for Batavia, arriving more than three months behind schedule with the usual report of arid and monotonous shores.

In 1629 the Dutch East India ship *Batavia*, loaded with chests of silver, jewels and silks, went aground near Houtman's Beach. She was a total loss. Her captain, François Pelsaert, was forced to leave 220 passengers and seamen on two rocky islands and take a pinnace and a skeleton crew to Batavia to seek help. Pelsaert followed the coast for more than 500 miles, accumulating the most detailed information thus far on New Holland's northwestern shores. He concluded that it was an "accursed earth." It had no harbors or good landings, and its drab terrain was relieved only by anthills so huge that he took them at first for the homes of the "Indians" he observed lurking about. Furthermore, the land was also the breeding ground for great multitudes of flies that "perched on our mouths and crept into our eyes." His woeful catalogue of the local fauna included one item that was of genuine interest, however—"a species of cat, very strange," with a tiny head and long hind legs. Pelsaert had discovered the kangaroo.

When Pelsaert returned four months later to rescue the survivors of the *Batavia*, he found that some of them had looted the wrecked ship and massacred those men who had refused to join in a scheme to capture the rescue ship and embark on a career of piracy. Pelsaert and his new crew managed to overpower the mutineers—most of whom they summarily executed—and recover a good portion of the cargo. The captain then sailed back to Java, marooning two criminals whose lives he had spared, in the pious hope that "God grant" they might be recovered at some future date with "trustworthy information about these parts." For decades Dutch captains sailing in the area were instructed to look for the pair, but the hapless mutineers were never seen again.

No further Dutch exploration of New Holland—voluntary or involuntary—occurred until 1636, when Anthony van Diemen, a leader of rare enterprise and ability, became Governor General of Batavia. Little is known about van Diemen's personal life. He reputedly came out to the East Indies under an assumed name, fleeing his creditors. In Batavia Coen took him on as a clerk. In swift succession he became a member of the company's local governing council, then its director-general and finally—after also being made an admiral of the fleet—the head of the company's entire Eastern operation. Van Diemen wielded his authority with more imagination and enterprise than any of his predecessors. He had a nimble mind that could attend to meticulous detail at one moment and to geopolitical strategy a moment later. He had read the Quirós memorials and felt the Dutch should continue to search for Terra Australis. Most important of all, he had the forcefulness and eloquence needed to convince company managers back in Amsterdam that continued exploration was in their interests.

As soon as he took office, van Diemen gave orders for a mission of

Words scratched on a flattened pewter plate record the arrival of Dutch navigator Dirk Hartog at an island off the coast of western Australia on October 25, 1616. Hartog nailed the makeshift tablet to a post, and another Dutch expedition found it still in place 81 years later.

discovery. He wanted to clear up once and for all the mystery of the southern New Guinea shoreline east of the point where the *Duyfken* had turned south toward Cape York Peninsula. He directed the commander of this expedition to follow the coast until he discovered whether it formed a closed gulf (the Dutch had already named the unexplored body of water there the Gulf of Carpentaria, after another governor general) or opened up into a strait. The expedition came to nought: Its commander was killed by Melanesian tribesmen in New Guinea only 11 days after the mission got under way, and his men soon returned to Batavia.

Van Diemen next looked toward the North Pacific, sending out two ships to locate a pair of islands reputed to lie east of Japan. Spanish vessels had once been driven there in a storm, and it was said that "gold and silver were almost to be picked up at discretion on the shore." The explorers failed to find the islands and lost almost half their crew to scurvy, but they made detailed observations of the Japanese coast and the Bonin Islands southeast of Japan. Perhaps the most significant result of the voyage, however, was that it brought to van Diemen's attention the man who was to fulfill the Governor General's goals for Pacific exploration. This excellent mariner was Abel Tasman, the second-in-command of the North Pacific exercise.

Born in a small village in the north of Holland in 1603, Tasman was intelligent and ambitious, distinguishing himself when young by learning to write—a rare accomplishment for someone of his humble background. In 1633 he shipped out to the Indies in the service of the company, and there he rose rapidly. Within a year he was a skipper, and in 1635 he was put in charge of a fleet of vessels engaged in harassing the shipping of the company's competitors, whether British, Spanish or Portuguese. Tasman proved himself capable of executing any task he was set—searching for smugglers, recapturing stolen ships, enforcing blockades, plotting safe trade routes, transmitting intelligence and chastising unruly local populations. The man was dependable.

The voyage to Japan gave Tasman a taste for exploration. This pleased the company directors who, prodded by van Diemen, were fast developing a taste for it themselves. But for the next three years, while they polished plans for a major expedition to the south, they kept Tasman occupied with a variety of routine company chores. Van Diemen, meanwhile, engaged a pilot whose abilities neatly complemented his own executive talents and Tasman's seafaring capabilities. Frans Visscher, a veteran of 20 years' service in the Indies, was considered by the company to have "greater skill in the surveying of coasts and the mapping out of lands than any of the steersmen present in these parts."

Early in 1642 Visscher produced a work entitled *Memoir Touching the Discovery of the Southland*—a remarkable document that provided the basis for Tasman's subsequent instructions. Visscher offered a number of different schemes for searching out the fabled continent, presenting them in ascending order of scope and difficulty. He started off with the suggestion that, to cover a large area, a survey of the Southern seas begin not at Batavia but at the island of Mauritius, 3,400 miles to the southwest, in the Indian Ocean. The ships should leave Mauritius no later than the 1st of October, to take advantage of the long summer days of the

Southern Hemisphere, "since at that time one may sail on day and night quite boldly." He proposed that the ships probe southward to lat. 52° or thereabouts and then, if no land was sighted, head east until they reached the estimated longitude of eastern New Guinea. Then, in the unlikely event that the quest still had not been fulfilled, they could sail north around New Guinea and come home, or they could extend their eastward passage along the 52° line as far as the assumed longitude of the Solomons and, at that point, head north, where "we do not in the least doubt that divers strange things will be revealed to us."

Those options were modest compared with what came next in his list of suggestions. A voyage of discovery, Visscher noted, could take in an even larger slice of the Southern ocean if the ships started from Holland, sailed to the Cape of Good Hope, headed south to 52° and then proceeded east; they could include in such a sweep the claimed discoveries of Schouten and Le Maire by sailing all the way to Staten Land, and then continue on across the South Atlantic for good measure. Yet another possibility was for the Dutch to establish a refitting station in Chile so that ships could depart from there on the old Spanish route to the Solomons, where they could take on provisions, sail south to 50° or so and

Mutineers from the shipwrecked Dutch trader Batavia (foreground) massacre their comrades in the Abrolhos Islands off Australia in 1629. Their captain, François Pelsaert, had set off in a pinnace to seek help for the stranded party; the mutineers planned to kill him upon his return, seize the rescue ship and go pirating. But when Pelsaert got back he captured the killers and executed most of them.

then catch the great westerlies back toward South America. Perhaps the best option of all would be to adopt several of these plans. That way, said Visscher, the Dutch would cover "the southern portion of the world all around the globe, and find out what it consists of, whether land, sea, or icebergs, all that God has ordained there."

Van Diemen admired the vigor of Visscher's imagination, but he also appreciated the dangers of trying to do too much too soon. The Governor General decided to concentrate on the first of the proposals and laid plans for an expedition—to be led by Tasman, with Visscher along as pilot major—which would begin exploring the South Pacific from Mauritius. The opening paragraphs of van Diemen's instructions to Tasman echoed Quirós, asserting the virtual certainty that a Southern continent of "fruitful and rich lands" existed; "thus it is certainly to be hoped that the outlay and trouble that must be incurred in the discovery of so large a part of the world can be recompensed with certain fruits of gain and undying fame." Visscher's scheme was to be followed almost exactly: Tasman's instructions were to head south from Mauritius to about lat. 52°, then to turn east and sail to the longitude of New Guinea—or farther if he judged that such a course was promising. Then he was to head north, find the Solomons if possible and come back around the north side of New Guinea to Java.

He was further told to keep his eye out for a short southern route to Chile, where the Dutch could "snatch rich booty from the Castilian, who would never dream of our ships coming that way." If time permitted, he could then come around to the southern coast of New Guinea to explore the Gulf of Carpentaria and the north coast of New Holland. And he was given one other major option. Instead of sailing east along the 52° line all the way to the longitude of New Guinea, he could turn north when he reached the longitude of the islands of St. Francis and St. Peter and investigate the as yet unseen eastern coast of New Holland from there. But he was to be back in Batavia the following summer. It was a fearfully tight schedule.

Tasman was given two ships, the 60-ton *Heemskerck*, carrying 60 men, and the 100-ton *Zeehaen*, a flute that carried 50. They were provisioned for 12 months and equipped with a remarkable array of goods for trading with the Terra Australis inhabitants: blankets, linens, chintzes, silks, 500 small Chinese mirrors, 200 pounds of ironmongery, 50 Chinese needles and one large brass basin. Tasman began his journal by noting that they sailed from Batavia "for the discovery of the unknown southland in the year of our Lord 1642, the 14th of August. May God Almighty vouchsafe His blessing on this work. Amen."

They arrived in Mauritius after a passage of only 22 days, putting them a week ahead of schedule. But on the way the crew of the *Zeehaen* had found that their ship needed extensive refitting. The expedition was held up for more than a month while the flute's rotten timbers and rigging were replaced. Tasman finally sailed—"God be praised," he wrote—on October 8, about a week behind schedule. Within two weeks, grass and rockweed were spotted in the water, suggesting land was near. Tasman posted a man at the masthead to watch for shoals. He promised three pieces of eight and a measure of spirits to anyone sighting land, but

none was seen. At the end of October the ships encountered hail and snow, and despite the advent of summer the weather was so dark and foggy that they felt it was "hardly possible to survey known shores, let alone to discover unknown land." On November 6 they reached lat. 49° 4′ S., and Tasman wrote that "the sea ran very high, and our men began to suffer badly from the severe cold."

That day Visscher formally proposed that they amend their plans. It now seemed fruitless to continue to 52°, and he suggested that they go back to 44° and then follow this line to approximately the longitude of St. Francis and St. Peter. From there they could go north to the latitude of those islands, east to the estimated longitude of the Solomons and then north again until the Solomons were reached.

Tasman put the question to the council of officers on the *Heemskerck;* by company policy all major decisions had to be ratified by such a council. The officers readily agreed to the change of plans. (Later generations would learn that if they had continued on the original course they would have found, with luck, only one dot of land, tiny Heard Island in the southern Indian Ocean.) To get the decision ratified by all the expedition's officers, the men on the *Heemskerck* set adrift a wooden case that enclosed the advice, to be picked up by the *Zeehaen*. The flute's officers signaled their agreement by hoisting a flag. By November 9 the two ships had reached 44°.

For eight days they pounded eastward into uncharted waters, propelled by the powerful prevailing winds and averaging 125 miles a day. But when they passed the estimated longitude of St. Francis and St. Peter on November 17, Visscher for some reason chose not to head north to investigate the islands. He stuck to his original scheme, and the expedition continued eastward. On the 24th of November, after scudding almost 5,000 miles east from the longitude of Mauritius, the explorers sighted a mountainous land. "This land being the first we have met with in the South Sea," wrote Tasman, "and not known to any European nation, we have conferred on it the name of Anthony van Diemen's Land in honor of the Honorable Governor General, our illustrious master." He had come to the west coast of the big island south of Australia that later was to be renamed for him—Tasmania.

The two ships beat their way down the coastline, looking for anchorage; but not until five days later, after rounding a southern promontory, did they come to a bay that seemed promising. "We had nearly got into the bay," said Tasman, "when there arose so strong a gale that we were obliged to take in sail, and to run out to sea again." The gale drove them up the east coast, and three more days passed before they were finally able to drop anchor. The following morning Tasman sent Visscher ashore with 10 men to reconnoiter. The group came back with samples of vegetables—and a mixed report. The land was high but level, well timbered but uncultivated. They had found just one meager stream. They had not seen any humans but had observed plenty of signs of human habitation, some quite mystifying. Smoke rose here and there in the distance, and the bases of trees seemed to have been burned out for fireplaces. They thought they had heard voices, and they had dimly detected the sound of a small gong. The trunks of two large trees bore notches at five-foot vertical intervals; these notches looked distinctly like steps, and Tasman wrote in his journal, "There can be no doubt that there must be men here of extraordinary stature."

The next day Tasman attempted to go ashore to take formal possession of the territory. A stiff wind and high surf prevented him from landing, and so he ordered his carpenter to swim to the beach to plant a flag. Then "we pulled back to the ships, leaving the above mentioned as a memorial for those who shall come after us, and for the natives of this country, who did not show themselves, though we suspect some of them were at no great distance and closely watching our proceedings." The explorers tried to continue up the east coast, but the wind was dead ahead, forcing them to tack constantly. Once again a council of officers was summoned, and they decided to turn to the east, resuming the course they had been following before coming upon Van Diemen's Land. The imperturbable

Tasman then sailed away from his discovery, having tried neither to apprehend any of its supposedly giant inhabitants nor to discover whether the land was, as he suspected, part of New Holland. His "illustrious master" would later criticize him for these lapses.

After a week's good sailing, the lookouts sighted another "large, high land" some 60 miles southeast of the ships. Tasman immediately steered for it, and the next day he was close enough to see surf breaking on the shore. Inland, mountains that later generations would call the Southern Alps towered so high that their tops were obscured by clouds. Tasman had made his most important discovery. He had arrived at the south island of the territory that would later be named New Zealand. He headed north along its inhospitable-looking west coast, making detailed notes and sketches of the shore's features. The land seemed desolate.

After three days the ships rounded a point—now known as Cape Farewell—to find a large open body of water. Coming upon a small bay that opened off it, they entered and dropped anchor. Smoke rising from the shore gave notice of habitation, and at sunset two canoes approached, their occupants calling out in "rough hollow" voices and blowing on a trumpet-like instrument. The Dutch responded with trumpet calls of their own. Then darkness fell and the canoes returned to shore. Tasman instructed the watch for the night to be alert, and to have their weapons at the ready.

Bulbous-hulled flutes, the work horses of Holland's maritime commerce, ride at anchor in a Dutch harbor in this 17th Century etching. Constructed with flat bottoms to keep them from running aground in shallow waters off Holland, the cargo ships proved well suited for negotiating the shoals of the Pacific.

Tasman's bold circuits of an island realm

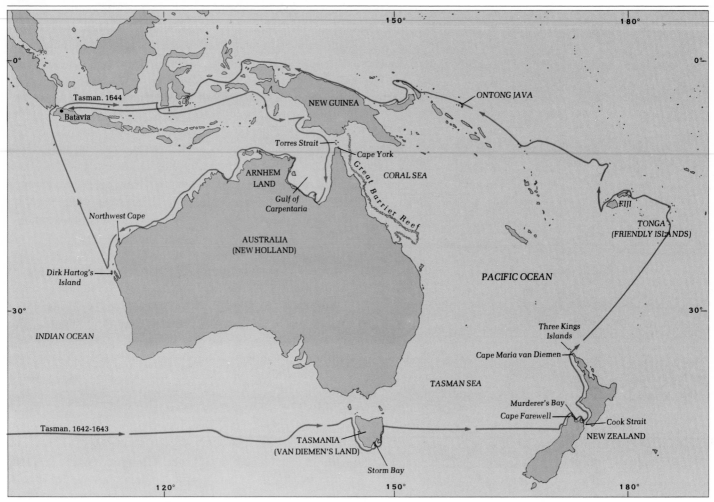

The next morning another craft came out—a double-hulled canoe whose occupants propelled it swiftly through the water with long, pointed paddles. Tasman reported that the men were of ordinary height, strong-boned, brown to yellow in skin color, with black hair tied in a tuft surmounted by a white feather. Thus did the Maoris—a Polynesian people who had settled New Zealand some eight centuries earlier—first become known to Europeans.

The Dutch tried to lure them aboard the ships with offers of linens and knives, but to no avail. Seven more boats put out from shore; two of them were very large, with pointed bows. One of these stationed itself between the two ships while another circled around behind the *Heemskerck*. The Dutch noticed that the Maoris were calling to each other and signaling with their paddles. A quartermaster and six other men set out in a cockboat to warn the *Zeehaen* against taking too many local people on board. When the small boat was about halfway between the two ships, the Maoris suddenly sprang into action.

"Those in the nearest canoe," Tasman later recalled, "began to paddle furiously. They struck the cockboat so hard that it got a violent lurch, upon which the foremost man in this canoe of villains thrust a long,

In 1642, sailing across the Indian Ocean and the western Pacific on a more southerly course than any previous explorer, Abel Tasman discovered the island later named for him, as well as New Zealand, before heading north into the Tongas and then home to Batavia. Two years later he traced 2,600 miles of Australia's northern coast from Cape York Peninsula to Northwest Cape.

blunt pike into the neck of the quartermaster several times with so much force that the poor man fell overboard. Upon this the other natives, with short, thick clubs and with their paddles, fell upon the men in the cock-boat." Three of the Dutch were killed instantly, and a fourth died of his wounds soon afterward. The others—including the battered quarter-master—desperately swam back to their ship. The Dutch fired at the Maoris, but the canoes sped off to safety.

Infuriated, Tasman's men continued to fire at any canoes that subsequently ventured toward the ships, but none came within range. The Dutch did not pursue the Maoris to shore and had to be content with giving the site of the skirmish the bitter name Murderer's Bay (now known as Golden Bay).

By this time they had seen enough of the land to realize that it was sizable. In a magnificent display of faith in the Southern continent theory, Tasman declared this place to be part of the Staten Land Schouten and Le Maire had seen off Cape Horn, even though that coast was more than 5,000 miles away.

But even if this was the unknown continent, it might be crossed by a passage leading to the South Seas and Chile. In hopes of finding such a connection, Tasman sailed out of Murderer's Bay and headed east, but "to our great regret" ran into squalls and a swift-running tide from the southeast. He tacked back and forth for several days but made little headway. Finally the council of officers decided the expedition should pull out of the troublesome body of water, head west to the open seas and resume its northward course. Had the ships continued eastward, they would have sailed through the passage (later named Cook Strait) between New Zealand's two islands.

The two ships continued up the west coast of "Staten Land," searching without success for another possible passageway to Chile. On January 4, 1643, Tasman arrived at the land's northwest cape—which he named for Maria van Diemen, the Governor General's wife—and sighted an island beyond it. Because January 4 was the eve of Twelfth-night, the Christmas-time celebration commemorating the visit of the three Wise Men, he named the isle Three Kings Island. (The name was later applied to the small island group that included this isle.)

Tasman decided to put into Three Kings for water. Trying to go ashore in a boat, Visscher saw a freshet tumbling down a mountainside, but the surf was too heavy to permit a landing. He and his men spied 30 to 35 extremely tall warriors on the surrounding hills. These Maoris carried clubs and "took enormous strides" while threatening the Dutchmen "in a very loud, rough voice." The same kind of demonstration was repeated the following day, and this time the surf was higher. Tasman assembled his officers, who agreed with him that they could not risk men and equipment in further attempts to land. They decided to proceed east to the estimated longitude of Le Maire's Hoorn Islands, strike north to them and then consider turning west to search for the Solomons. On January 6 the expedition sailed away from New Zealand without a single Dutchman having set foot on it.

For the next two weeks Tasman and Visscher navigated by hunch, groping their way to the east through totally unknown seas. On January

In a pen-and-ink drawing made by Abel Tasman for his journal, New Zealand warriors—manning canoes like the one enlarged in the foreground—swoop toward a Dutch cockboat between the ships Zeehaen and Heemskerck. The "detestable" attack, as Tasman called it, left four Dutch seamen dead.

19 they sighted land, a little island swarming with tropical birds. They had arrived at the Tongas—discovered by Schouten and Le Maire in 1616. Tasman, finding the inhabitants hospitable, spent almost two weeks there. With a lowlander's directness, he named the three at which he stopped Amsterdam, Middleburg and Rotterdam. The Tongans supplied their visitors with hogs, yams, coconuts and water in exchange for nails, beads and mirrors. Although Tasman complained that "the natives here are excessively licentious, wanton and thievishly inclined, so that a man had need of Argus' hundred eyes to look about him," he admitted that they cheerfully returned pilfered objects on demand. Furthermore, they were amusing. One chief, given a glass of wine, poured the liquid out and placed the glass on his head with a pleased look.

Tasman found some Tonga customs odd: Older women had both little fingers cut off, but younger women only one; the killing of flies (of which there were many) was prohibited; and a miscreant was punished by having a coconut cracked on his back. Marveling nonetheless at the general "peace and amity" of the islands, Tasman left on February 1.

His destination was the Hoorn Islands, but he failed to go far enough north. On February 6, as he tried to deduce his location, a strong southeasterly wind blew up, driving the ships toward a menacing group of islets and shoals. He had sailed straight into the treacherous Nanuku

Welcomed by islanders in three-man canoes, Tasman's ships lie moored off Tongatabu in the Tonga islands. This sketch depicts two other indigenous vessels: a fisherman's craft (right foreground) and a double-hulled canoe (left), with smoke rising from the stone-filled trough used for cooking.

Reef at the northeastern corner of the Fijis, a virtually impenetrable barrier several miles long. The *Heemskerck* and the *Zeehaen* were driven relentlessly toward a wall of surf, with no chance of turning back. Tasman surveyed the breakers and detected a small gap in them only two ships' lengths wide. He directed his vessels toward the tiny passage and they slipped through. "We passed between the rocks in four fathoms," he later wrote laconically, "though not without great anxiety."

The ships, now surrounded by shoals and more than a dozen small islets, were still in danger, and soundings revealed no bottom within reach for anchoring. During the morning Tasman and Visscher picked their way carefully through a maze of reefs. In midafternoon they spied an opening to the north and sped through it to safety. That evening a severe storm blew up. If it had come upon them 12 hours earlier, they doubtless would have perished.

Another council meeting was held to discuss the expedition's whereabouts. Visscher hazarded a guess that they were in the neighborhood of Quirós' Espíritu Santo, an island actually 800 miles to the west. But as Tasman wryly admitted to his journal, "the proverb that says guesswork often shoots wide of the mark may well be applicable to us." All the officers agreed that they should travel north to the 4° line, then west along the northern coast of New Guinea.

F is de plaets daer onse boodts liggen sude water halen.

G Syn du wonders vant lant soo als die by ons aent landt quamen met de hordanicheyt hunne cledinge Falzohs sude wezen

Sailing on, they ran into weeks of bad weather, and at one point were forced to heave to and ride out a storm. On March 22 they sighted a group of small islands whose heavy vegetation resembled the jungle of Java; the Dutchmen named the group Ontong Java. A week later they reached a land they assumed to be New Guinea (it was actually the adjacent island of New Ireland). From there Tasman easily made his way west along the known north coast of New Guinea. However, the ships' progress was slow, and they did not reach the western end of New Guinea until the end of May—too late, in Tasman's opinion, to continue around to the south coast and explore the Gulf of Carpentaria. On June 14, after a voyage of just 10 months, he arrived in Batavia smartly on schedule, concluding his journal with the words, "God be praised and thanked for this happy voyage. Amen."

Van Diemen did not—at least at first—consider the outcome so happy. Although Tasman had discovered two new lands that appeared very big, both seemed unprofitable. While he had made a "remarkable voyage," he had been "to some extent remiss in investigating the nature of the lands and peoples discovered, and left the main part of this task to be executed by some more inquisitive successor." In time historians of Pacific exploration would recognize the magnitude of Tasman's accomplishment: He had, after all, come a tremendous distance through seas

Inhabitants of the Tonga islands, clothed in skirts made of rushes, offer a woven grass mat and a fish for barter, in a drawing by Tasman. The Dutch were enchanted by their gracious island hosts, who allowed the sailors to fill their hogshead casks with water from an inland lake (background) where even the ducks, reported Tasman, "were not in the least afraid of people."

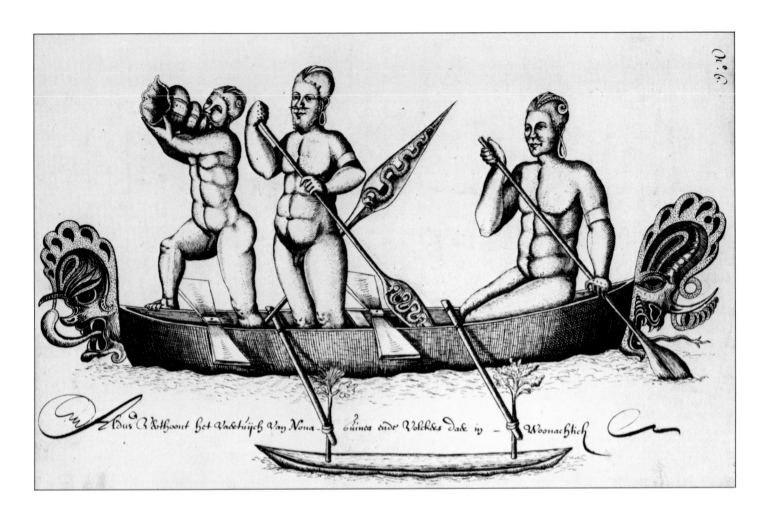

A New Ireland inhabitant trumpets a signal on a triton shell as his companions propel their canoe with serpent-patterned paddles. A member of Tasman's company commented on the boat's "elegant figures at fore and aft ends," which probably were intended as protection against evil spirits, and the curious "wing at the side"—an outrigger log with leaves still on the branches.

that were often perilous, had found and partly charted the coasts of Tasmania and New Zealand plus a host of smaller islands, and had kept to van Diemen's extremely tight schedule. And he had done all this with the loss of only 14 men—10 who died of natural causes and the four who had been killed in Murderer's Bay—a considerable feat in an era when it was not unusual for ships to return from long voyages with only a small fraction of their original complement.

Van Diemen himself eventually conceded that the voyage was more worthwhile than he had originally judged, and in 1643 he planned a follow-up expedition. Tasman and Visscher—both back in his good graces by then—were to return to New Zealand and resume the search for a southern waterway to Chile. But that same year hostilities with Portugal flared up in the Indies and compelled the Governor General to cancel the voyage. Instead, Tasman and Visscher were dispatched in February 1644 with three ships to complete the assignment on the north coast of New Holland that they had been unable to fulfill earlier. Tasman was charged with finding the answers to two lingering questions. First, was there a passage between New Guinea and New Holland? Second, was there a strait leading south out of the Gulf of Carpentaria all the way through New Holland to Van Diemen's Land or to the islands of St. Francis and St. Peter?

Although Tasman's journal of this voyage did not survive, his course can be reconstructed from a chart he made and from a report van Diemen sent to the company's directors in Holland. Tasman set out along the south coast of New Guinea and headed down toward Cape York Peninsula. Like earlier Dutch navigators, he was unable to detect any passage leading through to the east—an understandable failure, since the western approaches to the Torres Strait are masked by islands and shallows. He continued down the Cape York shoreline past the point the *Duyfken* had reached in 1605 and found that the Gulf of Carpentaria did not lead to a southern passage through New Holland. He sailed up the opposite side of the gulf, followed New Holland's coast all the way to its westernmost tip, then returned to Batavia.

Once again the ambitious van Diemen and his colleagues were irked. In addition to failing to find any new passages, Tasman had met—in their words—only "naked, beach-roving wretches, destitute even of rice, miserably poor, and in many places of a very bad disposition." The officers of the company were annoyed, too, that he had not gone inland at any point, since "he who wants to find out what the land yields must walk over it in every direction; the voyagers pretend this to have been out of their power." But the officials assured their respected superiors in Amsterdam that they intended to have everything investigated more closely, "by more vigilant and more courageous persons than so far have been used for this."

For unknown reasons the Batavia councilmen later changed their opinion, deciding that Tasman had given "reasonable satisfaction" and had "the courage to render additional good service to the company." They raised his salary and sent him off on assignments similar to those he had fulfilled before 1642. Meanwhile, they busily began to draw up plans for more voyages of discovery—only to have their schemes dashed by two stunning developments.

The first was an emphatically negative message from the managers in Amsterdam: They were not interested, they said, in discovery for its own sake. Exploration must lead to trade or to some other commercial advantage, and so far there had been no return on their investment. And anyway, they already had as many trading opportunities as they could handle, and did not wish to uncover markets that would simply be taken over by more populous nations in Europe. "These plans of Your Worship's somewhat aim beyond our mark," they wrote.

The second setback was the death in 1645 of Anthony van Diemen, the driving force behind all of Tasman's accomplishments. Only van Diemen would have been able to appeal the Amsterdam decision.

Tasman continued in the service of the company but undertook no more long voyages of exploration. On one occasion he fell into disgrace for a brutal act against two of his seamen: In a drunken rage he had attempted to hang the pair for flouting a minor order; the sailors were saved by another officer just as Tasman was slipping the rope around one man's neck. Tasman was fined, stripped of his rank and pay, and forced to make a public apology, but after 10 months the company restored him to active duty at full pay. In 1651, when he was 48 years old and a wealthy landowner in Batavia, Tasman retired from the sea. He died in 1659, leaving a bequest to the poor of his native village in Holland, and a much-improved understanding of the geography of the South Seas to the world.

Not all of his speculations were sound, of course. His theory that he had touched upon Staten Land during his first voyage did not last more than a year. In 1643 a Dutch captain named Hendrik Brouwer sailed all the way around Le Maire's discovery and found that Staten Land was only a modest island, not the edge of a continent stretching 5,000 miles west. Soon thereafter Tasman's find—the size and extent of which remained unknown—was renamed New Zeeland after a province in Holland (the spelling was later changed to New Zealand).

But by sailing between New Holland and New Zealand, Tasman had proved that New Holland did not extend indefinitely to the east, and in so doing he had irrevocably separated that land from the Terra Australis of legend. Tasman had also proved that no continent existed in the southern Indian Ocean, and he had charted the southwest Pacific more thoroughly than any of his predecessors.

Although the East India Company mounted no more expeditions, the Dutch did launch one final voyage of significance in the next century. This effort, curiously reminiscent of the mission of Schouten and Le Maire, was sponsored by the Dutch West India Company, which had a monopoly on Dutch commerce in the Americas. Since this franchise included the waters of the eastern Pacific, a well-to-do Dutchman named Jacob Roggeveen persuaded the company to authorize him to look for Terra Australis there. Roggeveen set out from Holland with three ships in 1721. He passed through the Strait of Le Maire and around the Horn. There he observed a great number of icebergs, and concluded that they had been formed on the shores of a Southern continent extending to the Pole. He found a new island in the eastern Pacific and named it Easter Island because of the date. In May he passed through the Tuamotu Islands, where he lost a number of men in a ship that was wrecked on a shoal one dark night.

By mid-June, when he reached the Samoa Islands, scurvy was rampaging through his company. The two remaining ships continued west and finally limped into the harbor at Batavia in September of 1722—to be met with precisely the same welcome that Schouten and Le Maire had been given 106 years earlier. The East India Company officials refused to believe that Roggeveen was not poaching on their territory. They seized and sold both his remaining ships and packed the company back to the Netherlands as virtual prisoners.

Although Roggeveen had not discovered the Southern continent, few thought that his failure, any more than the failures of so many others, was conclusive evidence that it did not exist. Popular opinion held that Terra Australis simply did not lie in Roggeveen's path. Nor, as Tasman had proved, did it lie in the western Pacific; New Holland, Van Diemen's Land and the islands discovered by Quirós were all clearly something else. There remained great reaches of unexplored ocean between New Zealand and the waters south of Cape Horn, and that was where the fabled land mass must be. But after Roggeveen's voyage, the Dutch ceased to look for it. It would remain for others to continue the quest.

A Frenchman's view of a curious world

The French were late-comers to the Pacific, virtually ignoring that ocean until 1700, when two ships under Captain Jacques Gouin de Beauchesne, an experienced naval officer, passed westward out of the Strait of Magellan. Even then, the foray was hesitant. Beauchesne moved north along the coast of South America, visiting scattered Spanish colonies and Indian settlements, and voyaged no farther into the Pacific vastness than the Galápagos Islands, 575 miles off the colony of Peru.

Beauchesne's expedition, mounted with the blessing of King Louis XIV, sailed primarily in quest of new trade, but—unlike most expeditions that preceded it—it also had another purpose: gathering information. A hydrographer by the name of Duplessis was assigned to chart the waters and map the lands that the company visited, and this scientist turned out to be an artist as well—a painter of felicitous if primitive talent who was fascinated by all that he saw. "I am joining useful things to curious ones as much as I can," he wrote, "and thought that I could please my friends while educating myself." The result was a splendid collection of watercolors depicting animals, people and places—with charming commentaries to match.

As a commercial venture, the Beauchesne expedition failed to pay its way, and it discovered no lands worth staking out for a French Pacific empire. But, owing to the presence of Duplessis, it was far more productive than that bare accounting would suggest. When he was not painting, Duplessis studied currents and winds and depths of anchorages, and charted straits, bays and ports in fine detail. His very appointment to the expedition reflected the dawning of a new attitude toward Pacific exploration, a turn of mind that he succinctly expressed in his journal: "It is necessary to notice everything in unknown countries in order to open a way to others and to oneself."

The French considered Duplessis's work so valuable that they kept much of it secret. But other governments were realizing the importance of scientific study, and later expeditions would carry astronomers, naturalists and ethnographers, as well as hydrographers and painters. The serious examination of the secrets of the Pacific had begun.

Watched by French sailors bundled up against the cold, women of Tierra del Fuego dive for mussels in the icy waters of the Strait of Magellan. "My drawings of their bodies and clothes are true to life," Duplessis wrote, noting that as the women dived they crossed their legs out of modesty. The letters on the drawing are keyed to his written comments.

Black-and-white geese swim serenely on a Tierra del Fuego lake.

68

*A penguin stands up as if for a look
at some distant object, while its cautious
mate keeps to the safety of the water.*

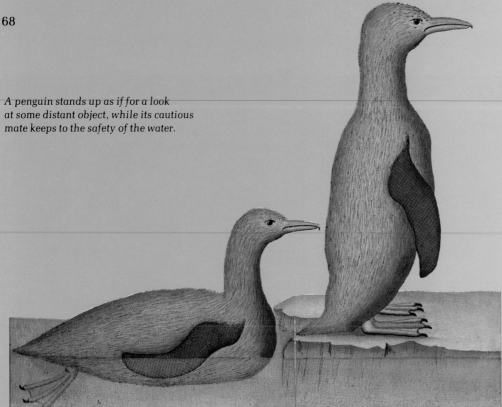

*Pikes at the ready, two French sailors
greet a sea lion on the Strait of Magellan.
These strange animals, Duplessis
wrote, were "the same size as a cow," but
their flesh tasted "like flavorless veal."*

A family of six South American Indians and their snarling dog confront a pair of French seamen in the woods of Tierra del Fuego. Duplessis sketched the Indians' hut diagrammatically, without most of its covering of skins, in order to show the bent poles that formed its frame, and the warming fire within.

A pair of South American Indians paddle out to sea in a craft that Duplessis said was "made of two long bundles of rushes tightly tied together from one end to another." As shown in his overview, slats athwart the bundles were the seats.

Steered by an oarsman standing aft, a log raft (below, in three views) carries Peruvian fishermen and their catch. Duplessis noted in his journal that the sail was woolen and the rigging was made of bark "as strong as hemp."

les Indiens de la mer du Sud nauiguent le long des costes suv sex Sortes de batteaux. dont il est venu a bord ce ne sont autre choses que deux grands fesseaux de joncs bien liez ensemble dun bout a l'autre. Suv lesquels il y a de petites pieces de bois qui seruent de Siege po'2 ou 3 hom. ainsy quil ce voit au plan A

mer du Sud ce seruent de ses Sortes de bastiments que nous appellons Ras
. . . iguent le long des Costes ou ils vont a la pesche il en vint vn a bord
. . . l ils a portoient du poisson a vendre, cette
. . . nem blage grossier de pieces de bois sans estres
. . . lles sont entaillées les vne suv les autres et
. . . ls la gouuernent auec vn grand auiron,
. . . ut decorses d'arbres qui sont presque autan
. . . aure la voille est dune grosse estophe de

Teüe en perspectiue du d. Bastiment a la voille Lorsquon est par le Trauers,

Teüe du d. Bastiment par le . . .

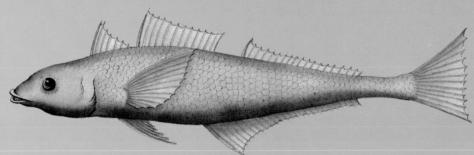

An 18-inch fish reminded the French scientist of European mullets.

Goatskins filled with air formed craft in which the Indians floated to Lima "as safe as if they were in a good rowing boat," Duplessis said. The vessels were inflated by a pipe—marked D in the drawing.

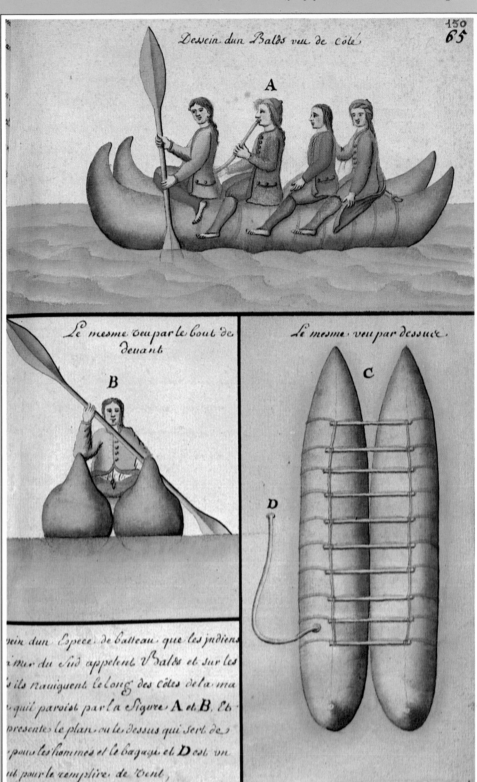

Brandishing a stick, a sailor prepares to club one of the
turtledoves that shared the Galápagos Islands' volcanic terrain
with other wildlife that showed little fear of man. The French
found the four-and-a-half-foot sea iguana (E) so hideous, Duplessis
wrote, "that none of us has dared to taste any of them."

Huge tortoises like these, some of which weighed as much as 500 pounds, were found throughout the Galápagos Islands—named after a Spanish word for "tortoise," galápago. The Frenchmen feasted on the tasty meat of these reptiles.

Duplessis thought the pelican "ill-smelling" and "not worth much."

Chapter 3

Intoxicating visions of a tropical utopia

t noon on February 20, 1769, Captain Philip Carteret, returning to England in His Majesty's ship *Swallow* after two and one half years spent circumnavigating the globe, was overtaken in the mid-Atlantic by a smart red and yellow frigate flying the French fleur-de-lis. The French captain slackened his pace long enough to exchange a few words with Carteret. Identifying himself as a M. Bougainville and his ship as the trader *Boudeuse* returning from Sumatra, he begged leave to send one of his officers aboard the *Swallow*. Carteret agreed—and was thoroughly baffled by what followed.

In the first place, the officer displayed inexplicable foreknowledge of Carteret's name and the name of his ship. Still more disconcerting, he seemed to know quite a bit about what the *Swallow* was doing and where she had been. He was aware, for example, that another British ship, the *Dolphin*, had left England with her two years earlier as part of the same expedition; that the two vessels had become separated shortly thereafter during a storm in the Strait of Magellan; and that the *Dolphin's* captain, Samuel Wallis, giving up the *Swallow* for lost, had proceeded into the Pacific alone.

At the same time, the Frenchman was full of pesky questions. He was particularly curious about the exact route that Carteret had taken across the Pacific, and constantly cast his eyes about the cabin as if he meant to remember every detail. "Oh, what a voyage for a ship to make," he exclaimed at last. Then, in an arch manner, he asked Carteret if he thought that such a ship as the *Boudeuse* could make the same voyage.

"I must own," Carteret later wrote, "that I thought this gentleman's questions & pert enquiries rather extraordinary, but attributed them to the Natural Curiosity of a Frenchman. I answered them all in such a general loose manner that he could not learn anything from me, which I imagine was a great disappointment to him for he then ventured to speak out plainer, and very modestly desired to know on which side of the Equator I had kept in crossing the Southseas. This I could not bear any longer, and getting up I asked him how he could presume to think that I should go and tell him my Voyage & added, my time is too precious to lose any more."

With that the conversation ended, and the French officer returned to his ship, entrusted with a packet of letters bound for France and a Polynesian arrow that Carteret sent as a gift for Captain Bougainville. The two ships then parted; the French vessel, said Carteret, "went by us as if we had been at anchor," and the *Swallow* plodded on toward England.

In this 20th Century rendering, scores of Tahitians rush across the waters of Hitiaa Lagoon on April 6, 1768, bearing welcoming gifts for French explorers led by the Chevalier Louis Antoine de Bougainville. Tahiti, wrote botanist Philibert Commerson, "is the one spot upon the earth's surface without either vices, prejudices, wants or dissension."

Carteret's mid-Atlantic encounter, more irritating than worrisome at the time, was in fact a classic instance of 18th Century international gamesmanship. In 1769 the rival powers of England and France were observing a nervous peace after the Seven Years' War by jockeying for position all around the globe. Although Carteret suspected that his French interlocutors had been less than candid with him, he discovered only later how greatly he had been deceived.

The *Boudeuse*, far from being a merchantman, was actually a commissioned ship in the French Navy. Her captain, the Chevalier Louis Antoine de Bougainville, was one of France's most cunning and competent military men. He, like Carteret, was on the last leg of a voyage of exploration that had taken him fully around the world. At ports along the way, he had learned a good deal about Carteret's expedition, and ever since he had left Batavia the previous fall, he had been trying to catch up with the *Swallow* so that he might glean additional information.

The explorers of the two nations had in fact covered much the same ground. Like Bougainville—and in advance of him—Wallis had come upon a large, strikingly beautiful island in the Pacific, a little west of the Tuamotu Islands. He had given it the name King George III Island and had tarried there, nursing himself and his scurvy-ridden crew back to health. After a month, Wallis' company had departed, never dreaming that the island would embed itself in the Western imagination as the quintessential tropical utopia—a balmy paradise free of human discord and designed for the perfect life of leisure.

True, Wallis, an Englishman, had discovered it, but it would not be the role of the steady Britons to promulgate the seductive myth of Tahiti—as the island's inhabitants called their country. Over the course of the next decade, the towering intellects of France would attempt to understand the implications of the new-found cultures of the Pacific, particularly Tahiti. These bewigged philosophs, as they styled themselves, eschewed much of Christian morality and harked back to the supposedly purer ethics of Greece and Rome. Many of them had long been seeking evidence of a contemporary society that was outside the bounds of Christian influence and was still, as they would have put it, "naturally" good. In an age of sumptuous banquetry and fervid sexual intrigue, the philosophs were thrilled by the thought of a simple meal plucked from bending breadfruit and coconut trees, and of human sexuality unshackled from the strictures of the Church. Pacific societies—and, above all, the Tahitians—appeared to be nothing less than a fulfillment of their theoretical ideal, and they claimed the island paradise as their own.

This surge of European interest in the Pacific represented a revival of sorts. More than a century had passed since Abel Tasman had entered the gut between New Zealand's North and South Islands in 1642 and returned to Batavia not sure whether he had touched an island or the coast of a new continent. The boundaries of the area still to be explored in the Pacific had not changed much since then; south of the latitude of Tonga, the map was blank for nearly 100° of longitude, from Cape Horn to New Zealand. And the east coast of Australia had not yet been seen.

The major exploring nations had, for a good part of this period, been

A rambler's best-selling adventures

William Dampier is portrayed with symbols of his travels.

The qualifications of the man chosen in 1699 to captain the British Admiralty's first South Seas voyage of exploration were, to say the least, unorthodox. William Dampier was best known as an ex-pirate and author. His book *A New Voyage round the World*, a brilliantly entertaining account of his adventures, had been published just two years earlier and was already in its fourth edition.

The circumnavigation that gave Dampier's book its title was a result of happenstance rather than design. Born into a humble English farming family, he traveled to Jamaica as a young man and worked on plantations and local trading vessels. In 1679 he joined a group of buccaneers, "more to indulge my curiosity than to get wealth." Over the next 12 years he drifted from ship to ship and ocean to ocean, all the while scribbling a record of his experiences—among them, dining on "A Dish of Flamingo's Tongues fit for a Prince's Table" in the Cape Verde Islands, and swimming a swollen Panamanian river while holding fast to a plugged-up section of bamboo that contained his manuscripts.

In 1686, while serving as pilot of a buccaneer vessel prowling the west coast of Mexico, he helped persuade the crew to cross the Pacific to plunder Spain's rich Manila trade. When rations ran low in mid-ocean, the men held Dampier partially responsible for their plight and decided they would eat him if the food ran out. The ship reached Guam with only three days' rations left.

The buccaneers soon abandoned all pretense of semilegitimate pursuit of Spanish prizes in favor of out-and-out piracy, which made Dampier resolve to get away from "this mad Crew." But the men refused to put him ashore, keeping him with them as they raided settlements throughout the western Pacific. Exacting some pain but little plunder from local inhabitants, they worked their way through the Spice Islands and even made a stop on Australia's northern coast "to see what that Country would afford us." Evidently it afforded them little: The first Englishmen to set foot on Australia left there unimpressed by either the land or its inhabitants, whom Dampier called "the miserablest People in the World." (Despite his sour assessment, the place was later named Dampier Land in his honor.)

In May 1688 the pirates finally marooned Dampier and seven shipmates on one of the Nicobar Islands, in the Indian Ocean. The castaways set off for Sumatra, 150 miles away, in a canoe that had a bare three inches of freeboard. Faced with "a lingring View of approaching Death" as stormy seas threatened to swamp the little craft, Dampier "looked back with Horrour and Detestation" upon his years as a buccaneer, and by the time he reached Sumatra he had decided to abandon pirating for good.

After working his way around Asian waters for two and a half years, he returned to England by way of the Cape of Good Hope, completing his round-the-world odyssey in 1691. When his journal was published six years later, the public's eager response and his meticulous descriptions of faraway lands and seas induced the Admiralty to select him as commander of the 1699 voyage to the South Seas. He proved to be an unwise choice: The expedition made no major discoveries, and Dampier's leadership abilities were so slight that after the voyage he was officially declared unfit to command a royal vessel again.

But even that did not conclude his rambles; he continued roving as a privateer and pilot. Before he died at the age of 64 in 1715, he had circumnavigated the world three times, had visited every inhabited continent and had written a total of four books that kept armchair travelers enthralled for generations.

too preoccupied elsewhere to search the South Seas in the name of either science or empire. Portugal was struggling to maintain her holdings in Brazil and Africa, while Spain concentrated on wringing as much wealth as she could from her American colonies. Holland was content to guard her lucrative East Indian trading concerns, and Britain and France until very recently had been too busy at each other's throats in North America and the Caribbean to give much thought to exploration.

One Englishman, an ex-buccaneer named William Dampier (pages 76-77), had led an exploratory expedition into the Pacific at the behest of the British Crown in 1699. An excellent navigator but a weak captain, Dampier discovered little. But he was a skillful writer, and after this voyage, as after others he made, he published an account of the strange lands he had visited and the remarkable sights he had seen. Readers marveled at such exotic bits of information as Dampier's report that shark meat "boil'd and press'd and then stew'd with Vinegar and Pepper" made a very savory dish, or his description of Bashee Island—one of the Batan Islands—where the inhabitants were willing to trade their gold for English iron on a weight-for-weight basis.

At about the same time, fanciful accounts of the Pacific had begun appearing in English fiction and belles-lettres. In Jonathan Swift's best-selling work Gulliver's Travels, the land of Lilliput was said to lie somewhere northwest of Van Diemen's Land. Daniel Defoe, sticking closer to reality, modeled his tale of the shipwrecked hero Robinson Crusoe on the true story of Alexander Selkirk, an unfortunate soul who had been marooned on the Juan Fernández Islands off the coast of Chile by Dampier on his first circumnavigation.

In France, the renewed fascination with the South Seas—and, in particular, with the fabled Southern continent—had taken on a more hortatory tone. "Who can doubt," wrote Charles de Brosses, a French intellectual and politician, "that such a vast stretch of land when discovered will furnish objects of curiosity and opportunities for profit to equal all that has been produced by America. How many peoples different from one another and greatly dissimilar to us in shape or figure, in manners, customs, ideas and religion must live there. What opportunities for trade in furs, silks, spices, medicines, dyes, gold and jewels. How many chances to sell our colored beads, our fabrics, our papers, our brandies and machines with as much profit as was gained in the first voyages to the East Indies."

The French were far from unacquainted with the South Seas. Indeed, they argued that a Frenchman had discovered the great continent itself—back in 1503, before Magellan had set forth. In that year an adventurer named Sieur de Gonneville had attempted to follow Vasco da Gama's track to the East Indies but had been caught in a furious storm and forced off his course. He ended up in a fertile country that he named Southern India and spent six months there. On the way home, his ship had been captured by an English privateer and de Gonneville had lost all his records, so that upon returning to France he was unable to say just where he had been. An account of the voyage published by a descendant in 1663 caused much discussion, and everyone tried to guess where de Gonneville's Southern India was. The best evidence is that he had

fetched up somewhere in the South Atlantic, perhaps on the coast of Brazil; however, his wishful countrymen placed the mysterious land in various locales ranging from the southern Indian Ocean to the waters south of the Moluccas.

In 1738 a veteran trader by the name of Lozier Bouvet persuaded the French East India Company to back him in an effort to find Sieur de Gonneville's Southern continent. On New Year's Day, 1739, sailing at lat. 54° far to the south of the Cape of Good Hope, Bouvet spied a high and rugged headland, which, because Christ was circumcised on that day, he named Cape Circumcision. For some weeks thereafter he was constantly in fog, but he was sure he had sailed along the austral continent. A devotee of the writings of Spanish explorer Pedro Fernández de Quirós, Bouvet also believed he had been close to Quirós' island of Espíritu Santo. As it turned out, he had stumbled across the most remote speck of land in the world. The nearest neighbor of Bouvet Island, as the tiny, ice-encrusted isle he had discovered came to be named, is Antarctica, 1,100 miles to the south.

Seventeen years later, in 1756, the polemicist Charles de Brosses was urging that Bouvet's discovery be followed up and that the French establish footholds in the Pacific. Perhaps they should start, he said, with a South Atlantic base in the Falkland Islands, strategically located just off Cape Horn, which would enable them to control access to the South Seas; then another advance base might be planted in the western Pacific, from which further inquiries could be made into the land and peoples of the great Southern continent.

Pacific-bound, British Commodore John Byron and men from his ships Dolphin and Tamar arrive in Patagonia, a South American region named by the Spaniards for the patagones, or "big feet," of its inhabitants. Byron described Patagonians as behemoths who made a six-foot-two-inch English officer appear "a mere shrimp" by comparison.

So artfully did de Brosses urge his point that he had the misfortune to be plagiarized. Ten years after his work appeared, a Scotsman named John Callander had the effrontery to bring out a tome that, despite his claim of independent authorship, was no more than a translation of de Brosses' proposals—except that wherever de Brosses had exhorted France to proceed on a given policy, Callander substituted the word "Britain." It was true that de Brosses' arguments applied to both nations. However, Britain, with its superior sea power, was more capable of delivering on them. And after the Seven Years' War ended in 1763, Britain was first off the mark.

In 1764 Commodore John Byron (grandfather of the poet Lord Byron) set out from England to do almost exactly what de Brosses had suggested. After stopping at the Falkland Islands, he sailed into the Pacific and all the way across it, without finding anything of consequence. He returned in May 1766 and had been home hardly two months when his ship, the *Dolphin*, was requisitioned for the Wallis-Carteret expedition, which was being sent out in hopes of settling once and for all the question of the Southern continent.

Sailing from Plymouth on August 21, the *Dolphin* and Carteret's *Swallow* arrived at the entrance to the Strait of Magellan on December 16. There they waited nearly four months, repairing and reprovisioning the ships. They set off again on April 11, and spent four more months battling their way through to the Pacific. In the process, Wallis lost

A noblewoman named Purea greets Samuel Wallis, commander of the first European expedition to visit Tahiti. The Englishman's stay was full of cultural surprises. Purea amazed Wallis by graciously lifting the ill captain over puddles. And when a British officer removed his wig, the Tahitians reacted, Wallis observed, as "if they had discovered that our friend's limbs had been screwed on to the trunk."

sight of Carteret's poor-sailing *Swallow* and decided to proceed alone.

Carteret also pushed on, eventually discovering Pitcairn Island, a coral-ringed South Pacific islet that he named for one of his midshipmen, and the Admiralty Islands off the northern coast of New Guinea. In addition, he was the first European to sail through the strait between New Britain and New Ireland, two islands east of New Guinea. Since New Ireland had never been claimed, he paused to take possession.

Meanwhile, Wallis had shaped a more northerly course and passed through the Tuamotu Islands, the 1,000-mile-long archipelago that had been discovered by Magellan in 1521. Wallis now gave its little flecks of land aristocratic names like Egmont, Gloucester and Prince William Henry Island. He made his landfall at Tahiti on June 18, 1767.

The Englishmen were treated with extraordinary friendliness by Tahiti's inhabitants, particularly the young women of the island, who were willing to accept iron nails as payment for their affections. After a month, during which Wallis had been forced to limit shore leave to prevent his men from pulling every nail and spike from the *Dolphin's* timbers, the expedition set forth again. From Tahiti, Wallis ran north and, picking up the North Equatorial Current, made his way back to England by way of the Ladrones, Batavia and the Cape of Good Hope. Upon his return he submitted a detailed report of his voyage, complete with a glowing account of the island paradise where he had been so well entertained. The Admiralty read it carefully, with an eye for trade possibilities and potential naval bases in the Pacific. Tahiti seemed likely to have a certain prosaic usefulness as a possession: Future British expeditions might want to stop there while searching out lands of real value. But for the most part Wallis' report was greeted with yawns—and worse was soon to come. Within a year his discovery would be claimed as a possession by another country, and the name Tahiti would become inextricably linked with another man—and a Frenchman at that.

Louis Antoine de Bougainville—cultivated, sagacious and humane— stood out as remarkable even in an age of exceptional men. He came to his seafaring career by a most roundabout route, one that included no formal nautical training. His father was a notary in the Paris Courts of Justice; his mother, who died shortly after giving birth to Louis Antoine in 1729, belonged to Paris' *haute bourgeoisie.* Because of her death, the infant Bougainville was taken into the household of a family friend, a wealthy and charming widow named Mme. Herault, who adopted him as one of her own children.

Mme. Herault's circle included the great mathematician and writer Jean Le Rond d'Alembert, who took a lively interest in the boy's education. When, as his father wished, Louis Antoine enrolled at the University of Paris to study law, he continued to pursue the strictly academic subjects that d'Alembert favored—linguistics, the classics and, in particular, mathematics. Such was his energy and intellect that he managed to succeed in several fields: After his graduation he was called to the bar, and a year later he published the first volume of a brilliant treatise on integral calculus that won him a place of honor in intellectual circles.

All the while, young Bougainville never denied himself the pleasures

of the city. A dashing *boulevardier*, he gambled at cards, enjoyed the company of glamorous women and indulged a passion for foils by attending an exclusive fencing school. His time crossing foils with the fashionable gentlemen of Paris was well spent; when the practice of law proved too boring for his temperament, he decided upon a career in the military and was quickly commissioned a lieutenant of the Mousquetaires Noirs, an elite regiment of swordsmen under the patronage of the King. Within the year he was appointed aide-de-camp to General François de Chevert, France's leading military strategist.

He was soon dispatched to the French embassy in London, where he cultivated friendships with many high-ranking British officers and carefully read the accounts of the great British naval explorers. Of particular interest to him were the writings of the First Lord of the Admiralty, George Anson, who had completed a circumnavigation of the globe in 1744 and was a firm believer in the strategic value of the Falkland Islands and the islands of the South Seas. The young Frenchman also regularly attended meetings of the Royal Society of London, England's foremost scientific association. In 1756, in recognition of his work on calculus, the Royal Society elected him a member—a signal honor for a foreigner only 27 years old. But hostilities between England and France broke out that same year, and Bougainville rejoined his regiment. In April he was on his way to America as aide to General Louis Joseph de Montcalm, the French commander.

During the successful French defense of Fort Ticonderoga, Bougainville was wounded in the head but insisted on staying at his post until

"A vast silence and a sad and melancholy uniformity," wrote Louis Antoine de Bougainville, greeted the settlers he brought to this remote bay in the Falkland Islands in 1764. The sailors and colonists built an earthen fort (foreground) before the ships departed. France claimed the strategic islands in hopes of restricting English access to the Pacific through the Strait of Magellan.

the battle was decided. For his valor Louis XV promoted him to colonel and made him a chevalier in the Order of Saint Louis. In 1759, after Quebec fell to the British and Montcalm was killed in battle, Bougainville returned home and was received as a hero at Versailles. But the idle life at court irked him, and he soon began casting about for a way to help his humiliated nation regain its respect and stature. Recalling the words of Admiral Anson and mindful of the admonitions of de Brosses, whose writings he had studied, Bougainville proposed a colonizing expedition to the Falkland Islands, then still unclaimed and untenanted. His friend the Duke of Choiseul, France's foreign minister, helped obtain the King's backing but could promise no funds: France was destitute. So Bougainville raised the necessary money from wealthy relatives and outfitted the ships himself.

With a group of 13 Acadians—French Canadians who had been expelled from Nova Scotia by the British—he set out on September 15, 1763. He was now in command of his own small fleet—a responsibility that awed him not at all, for he felt he had picked up all he needed to know about seamanship from books and by observing the officers on troopships to Canada. In February 1764 he landed in the Falklands and took possession, and the Acadians began tilling the bleak hillsides.

News of this bold move brought instant repercussions. Britain was incensed, alleging that English explorers had long ago claimed the place, and sent a naval squadron to reestablish His Britannic Majesty's rights. The Spanish were irritated: They considered the islands part of South America, a Spanish preserve. In the face of the joint outcry, France yielded—in favor of Spain and against arch rival Britain. Bougainville, who had by then returned to Versailles, was asked to dismantle his settlement and hand its title to the Spanish. Not one to enjoy retracing his steps, the chevalier requested permission to continue on into the Pacific from the Falklands. Approval was granted; the orders directed him to "proceed to the East Indies by crossing the South Seas between the tropics." The secret aim of the voyage was to acquire colonial outposts in the Pacific, and to probe for Terra Australis Incognita.

This time he did not have to pay for his ships. He was given the newly built 26-gun frigate *Boudeuse*, a smaller supply ship, the *Étoile*, and about 400 men. Two distinguished scientists signed aboard: naturalist Philibert Commerson to observe flora and fauna, and astronomer Pierre Antoine Véron to study new ways to determine longitude. Along for the sheer adventure of it was a dashing 21-year-old German prince, Charles of Nassau-Siegen, described as "military by tradition and dilettante by vocation." Surprisingly, Nassau-Siegen turned out to be one of the expedition's most valued members.

The *Boudeuse* sailed alone from Nantes on November 15, 1766—the *Étoile* was to join her later—and after two days at sea ran into violent winds that damaged her fore-topmast. Bougainville kept his vessel on course. But on the evening of November 18 the main-topmast gave way, and he was forced to put into Brest for repairs. With all the assurance of a seasoned mariner, he sized up the problem and decided the *Boudeuse*' masts were too tall for her hull. He ordered her masts shortened and her guns changed from 12-pounders to 8-pounders—another modification that enhanced her seaworthiness by making her less top-heavy. A much-improved *Boudeuse* left Brest on December 5, bound for South America. After accomplishing his sorrowful mission in the Falklands—the Acadian settlers were given the choice of becoming Spanish subjects or returning to France—Bougainville doubled back to Rio de Janeiro, where he met the *Étoile.*

Both ships needed firewood and supplies; but the local Portuguese Viceroy proved obstructive, and the expedition was delayed for many months. Commerson took advantage of the delay to collect a wealth of local botanical specimens. One day he came upon a beautiful climbing plant with showy red bracts and named it for his commander. Brought back to Europe by the expedition, the bougainvillea was to become a garden favorite around the world and make the explorer's name familiar to people who knew nothing of the achievements of the man himself.

On November 14, 1767—almost a year after the *Boudeuse* had left Nantes—the French ships got away from Brazil and set out for the South Seas. Bougainville elected to go by way of the Strait of Magellan, where snow, sleet and heavy gales assailed the ships, sometimes splitting their sails. At one point in his journal, Bougainville quoted—in Latin—the 148th Psalm: "Fire, and hail, snow and vapour, stormy wind fulfilling his word." In the ship's log he spoke more plainly: "Great wind, big seas." During calms he charted the coasts, and Commerson went ashore to botanize, accompanied by his valet, Jean Baret, who faithfully lugged the scientist's instruments, or by the Prince of Nassau-Siegen. Here and there on rocks they saw the carved initials of members of the Wallis-Carteret expedition, who had come this way many months before.

Bougainville himself went ashore for an interview with the inhabitants of Patagonia. Contrary to earlier reports, they turned out to be very friendly. "After many reciprocal caresses," wrote Bougainville, "we sent for some cakes and some bread from our boat, which we distributed among them and which they devoured with avidity." The Englishmen who had preceded the two French ships may have had something to do with the Patagonians' unwonted docility. "They appeared attentive to do what might give us pleasure," Bougainville said, "and by imitating the report of muskets with their voices, they showed that they were acquainted with these arms."

On January 26, 1768, after 52 days in the strait, the two ships ventured forth on the broad Pacific. Striking northwest, Bougainville began a systematic search for Terra Australis Incognita. He was looking for a coast that was supposedly located somewhere between lat. 18° and 20° S. Each day he allowed the *Étoile* to swing southward until she was nearly out of sight, thus expanding the breadth of their reconnaissance, and each evening the two ships rejoined and passed the night within hailing distance of each other.

But he found only insignificant islets covered with flowers and coconut palms. He decided that many explorers and geographers had deceived themselves. "Upon the whole," he wrote, "I do not know why our geographers insist that just on the other side of these islands begins a new land, 70 leagues in extent, that was, as they say, seen by Quirós. If any considerable land existed hereabouts, we could not fail to come

Sickly but irrepressible, botanist Philibert Commerson was driven by his self-described "mania for observing everything" to collect thousands of plant species while on Bougainville's global circumnavigation. In Brazil he found the bright-petaled vine below and named it bougainvillea in honor of his commander.

upon it. I agree that it is difficult to conceive such a number of low islands, and almost drowned islands, without supposing a continent near them. But geography is a science of facts; in studying it, authors must by no means give way to any system formed in their studies, unless they would run the risk of being subject to very great errors, which can be rectified only at the expense of navigators.''

The chevalier had pointed the way to a geological truth that would not be fully grasped until much later. Although the presence of numerous islands does often indicate a continental shelf below the surface and a mainland nearby, the South Pacific is uncharacteristic in having a deeply submerged sea floor from which great numbers of volcanic peaks rise just to or slightly above the surface.

Swinging north and then turning west, the ships pushed on for the Tuamotu Islands, which lay between lat. 10° and 25° S. In mid-February an epidemic of sore throats broke out among the crew. Bougainville had a vinegar tonic added to the cask containing the ship's drinking water, along with red-hot bullets to heat the brew. "At the end of March," he recorded, "we had nobody on the sick list."

The Frenchmen had now begun to detect signs that they were near land. On March 21 a big tuna was hauled aboard, and when its belly was cut open Commerson discovered half-digested fish of species that he knew were never found very far from shore. The next day the *Boudeuse* sailed close to a small island, whose inhabitants assembled along the

Prince Charles of Nassau-Siegen dispatches an enraged Brazilian jaguar as the animal claws the haunch of a horse ridden by the Chevalier d'Oraison, one of Bougainville's lieutenants. The German prince, who organized a hunt whenever the expedition stopped at a likely place, personally supervised the artist's work on this heroic painting of the episode.

shore, brandishing pikes in such a way as to make it plain that the Frenchmen were unwelcome. Bougainville named the place the Isle of the Lancebearers and judiciously sailed past it and the rest of the Tuamotu Islands without stopping.

For the next three days the *Boudeuse* and the *Étoile* ran due west in weather that Bougainville described as "the worst in the world." Squalls struck one after another, and rain fell continuously. Many of the men already showed signs of scurvy despite a daily ration of powdered lemonade that Bougainville prescribed, unaware that the vitamins had been leached out in the drying process. The firewood stores had been almost used up, and everyone and everything aboard ship was soaking wet.

On the second day of April, the skies momentarily cleared. Bougainville saw to the northeast what appeared to be a very steep, cone-shaped mountain surrounded by the sea; he named it the Peak of Boudeuse. To the northwest was another, much larger body of land, and he swung his vessel toward it, hoping to find anchorage there. Fitful winds delayed the explorers' progress, but they finally neared the shore on April 4. The ship was met by several canoes propelled by oars and single sails. One of these craft, manned by 12 naked men, seemed to lead the rest. As it came alongside the *Boudeuse*, the men in it stood and waved banana branches in a manner that Bougainville, drawing an analogy with the European olive branch, correctly interpreted as a sign of friendship.

The island was Tahiti. Wallis had viewed it nine months earlier with a certain degree of controlled astonishment; Bougainville and his company, on the other hand, were unrestrainedly rhapsodic. First of all, it was a vision of beauty. "The coast rises like an amphitheater, and the mountains are of considerable height," wrote Bougainville. "We could hardly believe our eyes when we saw a peak clothed with trees right up to its solitary summit. At a distance it may have been taken for a pyramid of immense height that the hand of an able sculptor had adorned with garlands and foliage. The less elevated lands are interspersed with meadows and little woods, and all along the coast there runs a piece of low, level land covered with plantations. We saw the houses of the islanders amid banana and coconut trees, and our eyes were struck with the sight of a beautiful cascade that came from high in the mountains and poured its foaming waters into the sea."

More wondrous, though, were the inhabitants. When the French ships warped into their anchorage in a bay somewhat to the east of the one where Wallis had stopped, they were again surrounded by canoes, this time bearing a great many young women. "Most of these fair females were naked," reported Bougainville, "for the men and the old women that accompanied them had stripped them of the garments in which they generally dress themselves. The glances that they gave us from their canoes seemed to reveal some degree of uneasiness, but the men, who were more plain, explained their meaning very clearly. They pressed us to choose a woman and to come on shore with her; and their gestures, which were unmistakably clear, denoted in what manner we should form an acquaintance with her. It was very difficult, amid such a sight, to keep at their work 400 young French sailors who had seen no woman for six months.

"In spite of all our precautions, one young woman came aboard onto the poop and stood by one of the hatches above the capstan. This hatch was open to give some air to those working below. The young girl negligently dropped a cloth that covered her and stood before all eyes as Venus showed herself to the Phrygian shepherd. She had the goddess' celestial form." Below, sailors and soldiers at the capstan bars passed under the open hatchway once on each complete turn, and Bougainville noted that "never was capstan heaved with such speed."

At that very moment the legend of Tahiti came into being: Here was the paradise of natural, sensual humanity. To the French voyagers, the coincidence was almost beyond belief. Back home, their countrymen were swept up in the theories of philosopher Jean Jacques Rousseau, who held that people in their primitive, natural state were good; only society corrupted. Tahiti seemed to be a demonstration that it was all true.

When the visitors went ashore they found the natives' hospitality so overwhelming as to be sometimes embarrassing. Invited to a house for a meal, a mariner would be offered a young woman, whereupon, said Bougainville, "the hut was immediately filled with a curious crowd of men and women," who "sang a hymeneal song to the tune of flutes. They were surprised at the confusion that our people appeared to be in, as our customs do not admit of these public proceedings. However, I could not swear that every one of my sailors found it impossible to conform to the customs of the country." The women were not even asking for nails. Observed Commerson: "Some censor with clerical bands may perhaps see in this only the breakdown of manners, a horrible prostitution and the most bald effrontery; but he will be profoundly mistaken in his conception of natural man, who is born essentially good, free of every prejudice, and who follows, without defiance and without remorse, the gentle impulses of instinct not yet corrupted by reason."

This utopia deserved a name that reflected its virtues, and Bougainville again evoked a classical image, calling it New Cythera. Cythera is the Greek island where Aphrodite, the goddess of love and beauty, is said to have risen out of the sea.

Given their general mood of rapture, the French were quick to forgive the Tahitian practice of pilfering—common among South Sea islanders. Not in Europe itself, said Bougainville, were there more "expert filchers" than these. Pistols, handkerchiefs and kettles disappeared mysteriously. An officer had his sword noiselessly removed from its scabbard by a bold islander coming up from behind. One day Bougainville himself was victimized. An old man visited his cabin and offered his three daughters in marriage to the chevalier. After declining and seeing the group off the *Boudeuse*, Bougainville discovered that an optical instrument was missing. He confronted the old man, who cheerfully gave it back. "No doubt," Bougainville remarked, "curiosity toward new objects awoke in them violent desires—and anyhow there are rascals everywhere."

Despite his inclination to see Tahitians in the best possible light, Bougainville suspected—rightly—that their society was not as simple and idyllic as it first appeared. Sexual customs were in fact complex: Unmarried women might be promiscuous, but not married ones. The

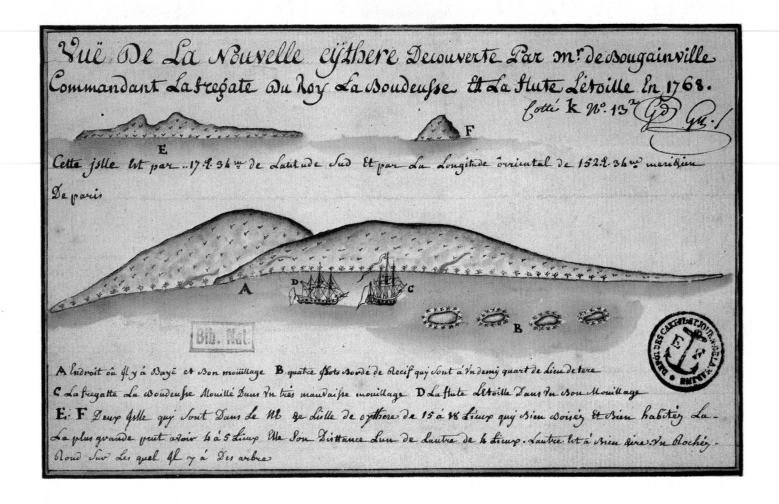

This "View of New Cythera," or Tahiti, which may be by Bougainville's cartographer, mistakenly locates the island at long. 152° 34' east (instead of west) and gives credit for its discovery to Bougainville—although the French explorer, who knew that Britain's Samuel Wallis had preceded him there, never made this claim himself.

Tahitians exercised authority tyrannically, made human sacrifices and practiced slavery. And they were constantly at war with other islanders, killing all the men and male children taken in battle and removing chunks of skin for trophies.

While the French were not cognizant of these darker aspects of the culture at first, they quickly discovered that Tahitian hospitality had limits. Soon after arriving, Bougainville made known his intention of setting up tents ashore for the members of his company who were suffering from scurvy. The local chief, Ereti, said the men could come ashore by day but must return to their ships at night. After lengthy discussions, the chevalier persuaded him to allow the afflicted men to remain in the tents. Ereti then asked how long the French expedition planned to stay at the island. Using pebbles, Bougainville indicated 18 days. Too long, said another chief, and picked up half the pebbles. For a time neither side gave in. Eventually a compromise was reached: 15 days. As a token of peace, Bougainville slept ashore with the sick men for the first night, and Ereti bunked there with him.

Still, it was not long before the delicate balance of good feeling was almost permanently disrupted by two regrettable incidents. In one, an islander was found shot; Bougainville could not find the culprit. Then three Tahitians were bayoneted by a group of soldiers from the *Boudeuse* during an argument over the purchase of a pig. Bougainville clapped the soldiers in irons; but Ereti and his people fled to the hills, and real trouble seemed imminent. Bougainville sent the Prince of Nassau-Siegen on a peacemaking mission, and with his charm and nobility of manner, the young man somehow managed to placate the islanders, who returned to their village.

After little more than a week on the island, Bougainville decided to cut short his stay, partly because he feared further incidents but also because the anchorage was unsafe. It was exposed to ocean swells, and a spate of bad weather had caused the *Boudeuse*' anchor cables to chafe and break. She had lost six anchors in all and could spare no more. Although Commerson was making valuable discoveries of fishes, birds and plants, and Bougainville could have used additional days to explore the island and survey the coast, it seemed necessary to go. Fortunately, nearly all the sick had recovered.

At the very last moment before departure, Ereti's younger brother Aotourou, who had become extremely friendly to the French, petitioned the chevalier to allow him to accompany the expedition back to France. Bougainville tried to dissuade him, then relented; the young man might help them among other islanders. On April 15 the ships left the magical land. They had been there just nine days. In all probability Bougainville had by now learned that the English had preceded him on Tahiti, but he nevertheless took formal possession of the island for His Most Christian Majesty Louis XV, burying documents to that effect near the French encampment. The explorer seems to have had a foreboding of the dislocations that the Tahitians would experience, now that their island was known to Europeans. "Farewell, happy and wise people," wrote the commander in his journal. "Remain always as you are now."

Aotourou hoped that Bougainville would stop at Tahiti's neighboring islands on the way west; he looked forward to introducing the French to the women there. But supplies did not permit a leisurely tour, and the ships headed on across the Pacific. Bougainville was following a course about 15° south of the Equator, and early in May he found himself among a group of islands whose inhabitants, on coming out to meet the ships, proved markedly less cordial than the Tahitians had been. They would not come aboard the *Boudeuse* and cheated repeatedly in the barter of food for trinkets. (Aotourou thought at first that this land must be France, since the local people could not understand him.)

Unable to reach shore because of the crashing surf, Bougainville named the islands (which he suspected might be the Solomons, discovered by Mendaña in 1568) the Archipelago of the Navigators, in recognition of the inhabitants' skill in canoe handling. In fact, the Frenchmen had touched a corner of the Samoas, the first Europeans to do so since Holland's Jacob Roggeveen nearly 50 years earlier.

The weather closed in, and for a fortnight the ships were buffeted by squalls and strong westerlies. Bougainville believed that thick clouds on the horizon usually meant the presence of islands, and steered his ships clear of these formations lest the stormy conditions drive him aground at night. "We were obliged," he recalled later, "to make way as if we were

Bougainville (seated) inspects some of the fruit that Tahitians bartered daily "for nails, tools, beads, buttons and a thousand other trifles that they looked on as treasures." The French captain repaid Tahiti's bounty in kind, leaving to the inhabitants a French garden of corn, barley, oats, rice and onions.

blindfolded, altering our course when the horizon appeared too black before us." The health of officers and crew was deteriorating again; scurvy recurred, and a new malady manifested itself—syphilis, apparently picked up in Tahiti. Just how this venereal disease got to the island has never been satisfactorily determined. Athough the Tahitians called the illness "the British disease," the English claimed Wallis' crewmen were healthy upon arrival in the islands. Similar denials were made by the French on behalf of Bougainville's company; just possibly the disease was already in residence.

Despite the storms and sickness, Bougainville continued to sail into the little-known waters to the west and west-southwest, hoping to find the large land mass reported by Quirós. Four weeks after leaving Tahiti he passed the Hoorn Islands, discovered and named by Jacob Le Maire and Willem Schouten in 1616.

All the while, Véron, the astronomer, had been reckoning the longitudinal progress of the *Boudeuse* by a new method, which he now used to fix the position of the Hoorns. Longitude was usually estimated on the basis of the distance a ship made good to the east or west each day. This calculation depended on a number of variables—including speed, wind and current—that could not be measured very exactly. The new technique, called lunars, involved making extremely accurate measurements of the angle between the observer's sight lines to the moon and one of the fixed stars—no small task on a rocking ship. From voluminous tables that provided the angles as seen from Paris (or, on British ships, from Greenwich) at every hour of the lunar year, the mariner could interpolate fairly precisely what time it was in Paris (or Greenwich) when he made his observation. By comparing this with the local time on the ship—which could easily be ascertained by shooting a star with a sextant and checking the angle against an almanac—he could calculate his longitude. Bougainville, using the old distance-estimating system, calculated that the Hoorn Islands were 179° 21′ west of Paris. Véron, working by lunars, came up with 180° 49′. The astronomer's positioning turned out to be almost exactly right: The Hoorn Islands are 180° 32′ west of Paris.

On May 22 two very large islands appeared; Bougainville named them Pentecost (for the date) and Aurora (because it was first sighted at dawn). Then other islands were seen behind these. The Prince of Nassau-Siegen landed on one with an armed party and was met by a crowd of Polynesians; all of them suffered from a skin disease, which later prompted Bougainville to name the place Leper Island. The inhabitants showed marked hostility at first, but they were calmed when the Prince, with his customary courage and aplomb, walked alone toward them and professed friendship. The party obtained bananas and coconuts. Bougainville came ashore that afternoon to take possession and buried the required documents at the foot of a tree, drawing on classical lore to name the islands the Great Cyclades (they are now known as the New Hebrides). As the party moved off, the islanders had a change of heart and showered the French with arrows and stones.

The chevalier sailed on among the islands and came upon a big bay on the eastern side of a body of land large enough to be taken as a

Sketches of Tahitian artifacts crowd a page from Commerson's journal. They include dugout canoes (top); and below them (from left), a poncho, a funeral compound with a platform for the deceased, and a breast gorget adorned with feathers and shark's teeth. In the next row down are Tahitian cabins and a beetle (right) for pounding cloth. At bottom is an ornament worn on a woman's forehead.

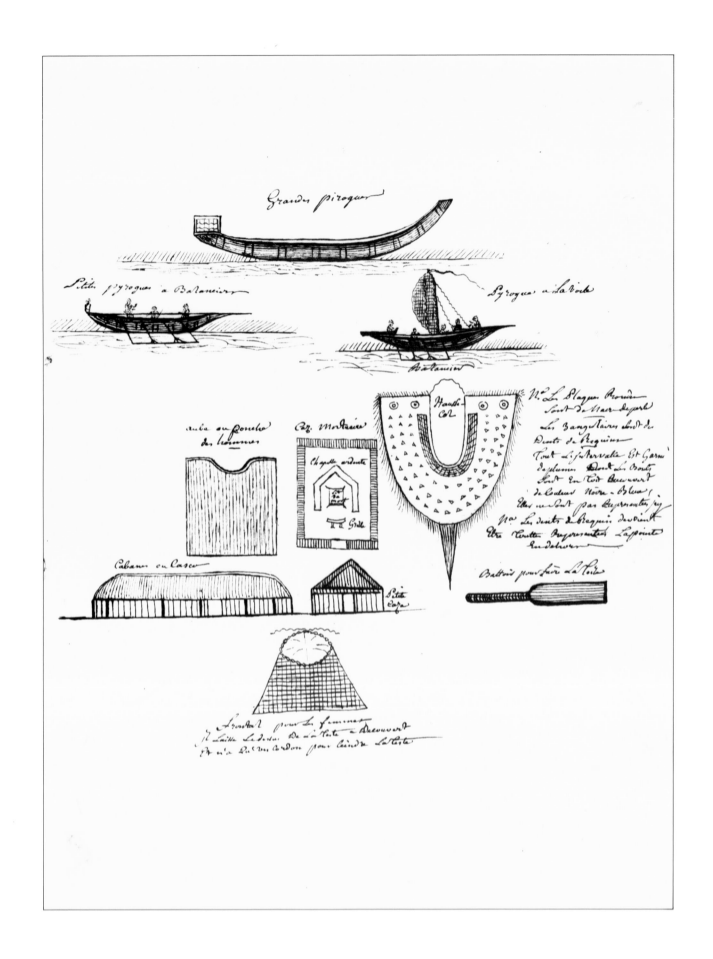

An international race for Pacific possessions

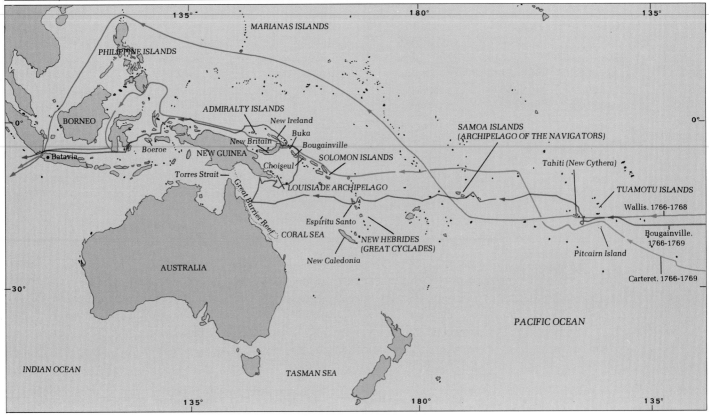

continent. Mindful of the work of Quirós, Bougainville doubted that the French were the first Europeans there. "Everything conspired to persuade us that it was the Austrialia del Espíritu Santo," he said. He was indeed in the group of islands discovered by the Spanish explorer 162 years earlier.

The inhabitants' intransigence had not changed in all those years. When a landing party attempted to go ashore, it was subjected to a hail of arrows, and the sound of drums was heard from the woods. The French discharged their muskets, but Bougainville bade them desist, "to prevent our being dishonored for the future by such an abuse of the superiority of our power."

While the ships lay anchored at the rediscovered Espíritu Santo, Bougainville had occasion to visit the *Étoile* and confirm a persistent rumor concerning Commerson's valet, Jean Baret. A hard worker and courageous companion, Baret had assisted Commerson in the wastes of Patagonia and the jungles of the South Seas, sharing his cabin on the *Étoile* and caring for him during the scientist's frequent attacks of seasickness. But something seemed awry. The valet was peculiarly furtive, shying away from the other men. And Baret's appearance was oddly delicate. Aotourou had hit upon the truth back on Tahiti: Seeing Baret for the first time, he had cried out, "*Aiene*," the Tahitian word for "girl." His fellow islanders had agreed.

Jean Baret was actually Jeanne Baret, a young woman of about 26 years, dressed in male clothing. When Bougainville confronted her, she

Separately, but with similar hopes of discovering new lands south of the Equator, English navigators Wallis and Carteret and French explorer Bougainville crossed the Pacific between 1766 and 1769. While bad weather, ill health and damage to their ships caused both Englishmen to swing north and catch the trade winds before completing their searches, Bougainville pressed on to the Coral Sea, altering course only when he reached Australia's Great Barrier Reef.

said she had been ruined by a lawsuit, began dressing like a man to get jobs, and signed on the voyage out of curiosity. Bougainville believed her and even commended her expressed wish to be the first woman to circumnavigate the world. But the truth—which did not emerge until much later—turned out to be rather different. Commerson was a widower and had hired Jeanne Baret some years back as a governess for his son. He had even mentioned her in his will—the same will in which, observers noted with a chuckle, he had set aside a sum to be awarded annually to some especially virtuous person. Quite simply, she was his mistress.

Bougainville recorded the revelation of Baret's sex impassively in his journal and assigned the parties separate cabins for the duration of the voyage. Journals of the expedition do not record how Commerson reacted to this, or indeed whether Bougainville ever spoke to him about the woman. "It must be owned," noted the chevalier, "that if the two ships had been wrecked on any desert island, Baret's fate would have been a singular one."

Delicacies resolved, Bougainville pondered his next move. Véron's observations, unquestionably accurate when made ashore, had pinpointed the location of many Pacific islands and had convinced Bougainville that the Pacific was quite a bit broader than previous navigators had believed. But other enigmas remained, most notably the question—almost ludicrous to anyone looking at a map today—of whether Espíritu Santo was connected to Australia, then known as New Holland.

To solve this riddle, Bougainville planned to push out to the west, knowing that the coast of New Holland lay somewhere ahead of him. Once he spotted it, he would turn north to see if he could cut between it and Espíritu Santo, thus proving the latter to be unconnected to the mainland. He was fully aware that he would be sailing toward the coast with the prevailing winds behind him—the classic lee-shore predicament. If he was caught in gales too strong for him to fight his way back to open waters, both his ships might be dashed to splinters against the coast of New Holland. "Little was wanting to make us the victims of our own perseverance," he noted, and set forth.

Luis Váez de Torres, of course, had sailed west from Espíritu Santo, satisfying himself of its insularity, and then threaded his way to safety through a reef-spangled strait north of Australia that was later named for him. The English knew the details of Torres' voyage, but neither they nor Spain had shared their information with the French. To Bougainville's knowledge, no European had visited the area he was about to enter. It was the large body of water now known as the Coral Sea.

Bougainville shaped a course due west along lat. 15° S. On the night of June 6, he suddenly found himself in danger. An enormous reef—known today as Australia's Great Barrier Reef—stretched off into the distance. "The sea broke with great violence on these shoals," Bougainville wrote, "and peaks of rock appeared above water here and there. It was the voice of God, and we were obedient to it."

Turning north, Bougainville disposed of the notion that Espíritu Santo was connected to Australia, but his new course did not lead immediately to safety. Three days later he sighted land, "extremely high in the interior, with magnificent lowlands along the seashore." It was

the south coast of New Guinea, and it sent a delicious fragrance across the water. Although he thought there might be a strait leading out to the west, Bougainville chose to sail east and then north to New Britain in hope of finding the food and water his ships now sorely needed. To do this, he had to battle three forces: a strong wind blowing up from the southeast, fast currents that swept northwest across the Coral Sea to the Torres Strait, and a ground swell that continually hove the ships toward the land. "The following days were dreadful," he wrote. "Everything was against us; the wind constantly blowing very fresh at east-southeast and southeast; the rain; a fog so thick that we were obliged to fire guns in order to keep company with the *Étoile*. Thus we were forced to make our way, in the dark, in the midst of a sea strewn with shoals, being obliged to shut our eyes to all signs of danger."

Provisions were now so low that a pet dog was eaten, then the ship's goat. Bougainville had to issue a ban on eating the leather off the yards. One officer caught a rat, which he shared with the Prince of Nassau-Siegen, observing wryly, "Happy we shall be if we can have one now and then, without the others beginning to acquire a taste for them."

In a few days the clouds lifted, but there still was no way to the north: Bougainville was beating his way along an immense chain of islets, reefs

The discovery of a new island group, the Louisiades, sparks a fever of activity aboard the Boudeuse on June 16, 1768. To the left of the mast, scarlet-uniformed officers look over the shoulder of a kneeling man reading the land's bearing on a compass. Sailors in the left foreground prepare a boat for launch, while others at right fire a cannon to alert the men aboard the sister ship, the Étoile. The painting was done by Louis-Ambroise Garneray in 1848.

and shoals that form the southeastern tail of New Guinea. At last, on June 25, he reached the end of the archipelago and turned north. The grateful chevalier named the place Cape Deliverance and called the string of islands the Louisiades, after Louis XV. "I think," Bougainville remarked in his journal, "we have well acquired the right of naming these parts." Previous navigators had "all followed the same track; we opened a new one and paid dear for the honor of the first discovery."

On June 30, after experiencing more bad weather, he came to a large body of land that did not appear on his charts. The ships approached a bay that seemed to offer good holding ground. But war canoes carrying about 150 men each—black, almost naked, with hair dyed white, yellow or red—threatened to give battle, and Bougainville decided against attempting to land. He called the island Choiseul, after the foreign minister who had supported his expedition. Years later, geographers deduced that it was one of the Solomon Islands; the chevalier had come upon Mendaña's archipelago without recognizing it.

Continuing on in search of New Britain, Bougainville "discovered to the westward a long hilly coast, the tops of whose mountains were covered with clouds." Off this land's northwestern shore was a small island that looked inviting. But when the two ships tried to anchor there, they were once again met by hostile inhabitants who refused to supply food and water. They named the island Buka—a word (the meaning of which has never been discovered) that the islanders chanted incessantly when they first saw the Europeans. He never gave a name to the larger body of land to the south, but a later generation corrected that oversight by naming it after the chevalier himself. Bougainville today is the westernmost island of the Bismarck Archipelago, a string of large islands scattered off New Guinea's northeast coast.

Two days later he reached what he assumed to be New Britain. Actually it was New Ireland, a narrow island 200 miles long adjacent to New Britain. There the voyagers found little to eat, and whatever fruit they gathered was generally covered with ants. Still, they were able to rest and patch the ships.

One day a sailor walking on the beach discovered, half-buried in the sand, part of a lead plate with some words in English on it. Bougainville ordered a search of the surrounding area, and not far away the vestiges of a camp were found. From the length of fresh shoots that had sprouted from the stumps of ax-felled trees, Bougainville and Commerson estimated that the camp had been made about four months previously. The lead plate was Carteret's memento of taking possession. He had nailed it to a tree, but inhabitants of the island had wrenched it off. Not to be outdone, Bougainville took possession too, certain that his government would expect it of him.

Torrential rains and unfavorable winds pinned the explorers to the spot for two weeks. The rains let up long enough to allow Véron to observe an eclipse of the sun and to derive the exact longitude of their anchorage—149° 44′ 15″ east of Paris. Meanwhile, Commerson collected bugs and plants, and the Prince went hunting.

At last, on July 25, the *Boudeuse* and the *Étoile* set sail. Swinging north, the French ships ran along the east coast of New Ireland before

French explorers on the island of New Ireland lounge beside Praslin Cascade in July 1768. The huge rock steps of the falls, said expedition leader Bougainville, formed "a hundred different basins, colored and shaded by trees of immense height." Despite its scenic appeal, New Ireland proved inhospitable, abounding in ants, snakes and scorpions, and offering little in the way of fresh food.

turning west to head for the Moluccas. All along this coast they were attacked by warriors in canoes. The French defended themselves vigorously, and one officer related that the assailants had to return to shore "carrying the wounded and the dead. Sometimes the water around their canoes was red with blood, and some of their canoes sank to the bottom, shot through by muskets and blunderbusses."

The worst enemy was still malnutrition. By late August there were 45 cases of scurvy, and on August 24 the disease caused its first death. "Each day," wrote Bougainville, "brings new victims. Good God, how terrible the food is. We must eat what ordinarily would be thrown in the sea. People have long argued about the location of hell. Frankly, we have discovered it." Yet under the chevalier's leadership the spirits of the group remained good, and every evening the sailors danced on deck.

Mile by mile the two ships made their way along the north coast of New Guinea, and finally on September 1 they came to a Dutch outpost on Boeroe, a tiny island in the Moluccas, 300 miles west of New Guinea. The Dutch Governor was under instructions not to allow foreign ships into his port, but after some negotiations the *Boudeuse* and the *Étoile* were able to anchor and obtain food. Bougainville recalled that his first meal ashore was one of the most delightful moments of his life. "One must have been a sailor, and reduced to the extremities that we had felt for several months together," he said, "in order to form an idea of the sensations that the sight of greens and a good supper may produce." After being entertained royally, Bougainville was somewhat surprised to be presented—as he prepared to depart—with a bill for all food and drink consumed by the company, as well as for provisions taken aboard.

Refreshed and with their sick recovering, the French moved on to the Dutch base of Batavia, where Bougainville learned the identity of the elusive Englishmen who had preceded him. He thought it would be interesting to catch up to Carteret, and for this reason—and to minimize the effects of the dysentery for which Batavia had become notorious—he sailed on October 18 for the French island of Mauritius in the Indian Ocean. There he had the *Boudeuse* overhauled and cleaned. Commerson, desiring to study the natural history of the island, left the expedition at this point, and with him went Jeanne Baret. (After the botanist's death a few years later, she returned to France, married and lived out her days in a quiet provincial village.)

Bougainville left the *Étoile* behind for further repairs, and sped on in the refurbished *Boudeuse*. At the Cape of Good Hope he found he was only a few days behind Carteret. North of Ascension Island he caught the Englishman, and delighted in the chance to greet him without revealing how close their paths had been. "His ship was very small, and went very ill," observed the chevalier. "How much he must have suffered in so bad a vessel may well be conceived."

The *Boudeuse* sailed into the French port of Saint-Malo in March 1769. She had been away for two years and four months and in all that time had lost only seven men, all from illness. The *Étoile* arrived a month later; she had lost only two.

Bougainville's achievements were numerous. His discovery of the Louisiades, Choiseul and Bougainville Island added significant new

Captain Hyacinthe de Bougainville, son of the great French explorer of the Pacific, leans against the rail of the Thétis, a frigate in which he won his own fame by sailing around the world from 1824 to 1826. Behind him are the sails of the corvette Espérance, which accompanied the Thétis on the expedition.

material to the map of the Pacific. His and Véron's careful observations helped define more clearly the blurred picture that 18th Century cartographers had of that area, and Commerson's botanical discoveries added significantly to his science's growing list of flora. More to the point, Bougainville had awakened French interest in the Pacific. Tahiti, the pearl of the Pacific, was to be the avatar of that interest, though France would not take clear title to the island until 1847 when, in exchange for concessions granted elsewhere, England withdrew her claims.

From the moment of the chevalier's return, all Paris buzzed with discussion about that enchanted isle and the South Seas. What really piqued French curiosity, however, was the chevalier's passenger, Aotourou—the apparent personification of a natural man: Aotourou was affable and soft-spoken, and though bewildered by Paris, he soon became devoted to it. He grew particularly fond of the opera and would attend performances alone, paying at the door and sitting in the gallery behind the boxes. He preferred operas in which there was dancing, and he delighted in visiting the ballerinas backstage. Nevertheless, after 11 months in France, Aotourou became homesick for Tahiti—to no one's surprise.

Bougainville had promised to ensure his return and now made good on his word, paying for the charter of a ship out of his own pocket—a gesture that cost him a third of his entire estate. Sadly, an epidemic of smallpox broke out among the ship's crew on the way out; Aotourou caught the disease and died before reaching his island home. Bougainville was blamed by many for Aotourou's fate. If the chevalier had not lured him from his island home, so the argument ran, Aotourou might have lived a long, idyllic life on Tahiti.

Such criticism stung, but it did not dull the chevalier's zeal for exploration. In the early 1770s, after finishing a book recounting his circumnavigation, Bougainville offered to lead a French expedition to the northern polar regions. But the government declined to back him, and his own funds were too meager to outfit the venture. When France joined the rebelling American colonies in war against Britain in 1778, Bougainville went to sea again. In 1781, while commanding a ship in the fleet of Admiral Count François Joseph Paul de Grasse, he helped to lead the successful naval attack on the British in the Battle of Chesapeake Bay, which set the stage for the great victory at Yorktown that sealed America's independence. He finally married in 1780—he was 50, his bride 20—and sired four sons, one of whom, carrying the felicitous name Hyacinthe, became a naval officer and participated in an expedition to the Pacific in the early 19th Century.

The elder Bougainville narrowly missed the guillotine as a Royalist during the French Revolution, but reemerged in his last years as a friend and adviser to Napoleon. Decorated and once again revered, he died at the age of 82 in 1811.

His modesty and humor had never departed him. In his old age he liked to recollect for friends a remark he had made upon returning from his great circumnavigation. Questioned about his many adventures, he had reached for the plant that Commerson had named for him and said, "Well, I am also placing hope for my reputation in a flower."

Polynesian voyagers: the first Pacific navigators

When European explorers first entered the Pacific, they found that the great ocean had already been mastered by navigators whose nautical skills rivaled their own: the Polynesians. The presence of the Polynesians throughout the ocean's constellation of volcanic isles was testimony to an extraordinary seafaring heritage. Starting from islands near Southeast Asia around 2500 B.C., their ancestors had island-hopped into the Pacific until they reached the Tonga and Samoa groups about a millennium later. There they perfected an ocean-oriented culture that lent itself to prodigious feats of migration.

When driven from an island by overpopulation, famine or defeat in battle, Polynesians would set off to colonize new lands—sometimes sending exploring parties ahead, sometimes simply trusting fate and their own arcane abilities to lead them to another home (they were not always rewarded; many expeditions perished at sea). Such long voyages were planned months in advance. Even islanders forced into exile by conquering neighbors were given time to build massive double-hulled canoes that could carry scores of people on journeys of eight weeks or more.

Building a voyaging canoe was a community project, supervised by a master craftsman of near-priestly status. Workers shaped large tree trunks into rough hulls and then, with primitive tools of stone, shell and bone, constructed a sturdy sailing vessel that could cover 150 miles in a day.

The canoes were guided to their destinations by an elite fraternity of navigators, taught from childhood to read nautical information in a host of natural phenomena. They knew the year-round positions of more than 150 stars and had a vast knowledge of ocean currents, prevailing winds and the habits of migratory birds. When nearing islands beyond the horizon, they could actually smell land, feel echoes in the water from swells bouncing off atolls and see the greenish reflection of forests on the underside of clouds.

Following such clues, the Polynesians crossed 15 million square miles of unknown ocean, and by the Eighth Century they had colonized virtually every habitable speck in a vast triangle bound by Hawaii on the north, New Zealand in the southwest and Easter Island to the east.

A wizened master builder (right) calks a partially completed hull with breadfruit gum before his workers stitch wooden strakes to its sides. At left, a man shapes a second hull with a stone adz, while his companion uses a drill with a shark's-tooth bit to bore holes in a strake. Finishing tools included the small pumice stone and bow-shaped rasp of stretched sharkskin in the right foreground.

The canoe's twin hulls, their sides sealed with a protective varnish made from nut oils, are lashed to the crossbeams that hold them parallel and support the plank deck. A voyaging canoe might be up to 100 feet long and—with its deck, thatched deckhouse, masts and rigging in place—might weigh 10 tons.

To make coconut-fiber rope, called sennit, an old man (left) strips fiber that will be soaked in sea water for eight weeks. A worker (background) pounds soaked fiber to soften it, and his partner (second from left) braids the pounded material into rope. Meanwhile, Polynesian women split pandanus leaves into slim strips for woven mats to be sewed into the sails.

A priest (rear center) chants ritual incantations as the canoe
is tugged down a log ramp—strewn with leaves so the boat will
slide easily—and into the sea. A launching was followed
by a night of feasting and then days of short shakedown cruises.

At sea, voyagers attend to their daily chores. Watched by a small dog—of a barkless, vegetarian breed that the Polynesians raised for food—two men haul in a tuna with a trolling line. In the foreground a bailer ladles water from a hull, while another man, in front of the cooking-fire sandbox, breaks coconuts open with a spike made from a marlin's bill. Bananas and food bundled in pandanus leaves lie among caged pigs and chickens that will be used as breeding stock for the new island.

At night the navigator stands on the
windward hull to see the guiding stars.
Wind direction is shown by a feather
pennant fluttering from a curved boom.

The successful voyagers settle into their new home—building thatched huts, gathering local food plants, making fishnets and repairing their canoe for use in exploring the shoreline. Coastal excursions were important to establish the group's claim to territory before other Polynesians arrived; some islands were settled by successive waves of migrants.

Chapter 4

The great ocean's greatest explorer

n April 3, 1768, the *Earl of Pembroke*, an ungainly-looking North Sea coal carrier, was put into dry dock in a choice slip at the English Naval shipyard of Deptford, on the Thames River near London. Stout and heavy-timbered, with a bluff bow and a narrow stern, the new arrival appeared distinctly out of place amid the rows of sleek frigates and towering ships of the line being repaired and refitted for duty. A few Deptford officers brusquely questioned whether the bark-rigged vessel was even mustered in the Royal Navy. For what conceivable purpose could the Admiralty require the services of a grimy workboat?

In fact, the humble collier was intended for a singularly adventurous role. She would carry a hand-picked group of naval officers and scientists to the farthest reaches of the Pacific to conduct vital astronomical studies and to make yet another search for the continent identified on the maps as Terra Australis Incognita. A collier had been selected because it could hold the large quantities of supplies and scientific equipment the voyagers would require, and also because it was flat-bottomed and was able to take the punishment of an accidental grounding.

On April 5 the Admiralty renamed the vessel *Endeavour* and ordered the Deptford carpenters to prepare her for the journey with the greatest dispatch. Within four weeks her hull had been sheathed with a second layer of planking to protect against tropical sea worms *(page 110)*. Her masts and yards were scrapped for fresh-cut spars, and all her rigging was replaced with new hempen lines. On May 18 the ship was refloated and moored in the great Deptford Basin, alongside the mighty warships of the British Empire, to await the arrival of her commander.

To some Londoners the selection of Lieutenant James Cook as leader of the expedition to the Pacific was even more surprising than the Admiralty's choice of the *Endeavour*. At the age of 39, Cook was virtually unknown to his countrymen. In marked contrast to Commodore John Byron and Captain Samuel Wallis, the aristocratic leaders of England's earlier voyages of Pacific exploration, Cook sprang from the lower ranks of society, was haphazardly educated and had not even spent his whole career in the Royal Navy: His training had been in the merchant marine.

But, like the *Endeavour*, James Cook possessed exactly those qualities deemed crucial by the Admiralty for the success of the job at hand. For four years, beginning in 1763, Cook had sailed the rugged coast of Newfoundland, charting its bays and inlets with painstaking precision. More than once he had earned praise from the highest levels of the Navy for his surveying work and superb seamanship, and the Lords of the Admiralty reasoned that the talents that had been so valuable in the Newfoundland enterprise would be equally useful in the uncharted waters of the South Pacific. As it turned out, Cook would become the greatest explorer of his time—and the greatest Pacific explorer of all time.

As captain of the *Endeavour*, he would sight and survey hundreds of landfalls that no Westerner had ever laid eyes on. And though the *Endeavour* would never fire her guns at another ship in battle, Cook's epochal voyage aboard the converted collier was destined to bring under George III's sovereignty more land and wealth than any single naval victory of the powerful British fleet. But the most important prize of this

Wearing an expression of unbending resolve, James Cook looks up from a chart in a portrait made three years before his death in 1779. The greatest of the South Seas navigators, he was posthumously awarded a coat of arms that was inscribed "He left nothing unattempted."

and the two subsequent voyages that Cook would make was measured not in territory but in knowledge. Patient and methodical where his predecessors had been hasty and disorganized, he would sweep away myths and illusions on a prodigious scale, and in the end would give to the world a long-sought treasure: a comprehensive map of the Pacific.

Cook's achievements were all the more remarkable in that his forebears had evinced no interest whatsoever in the sea. Born in the Yorkshire village of Marton-in-Cleveland on October 27, 1728, he was the second son of a farm laborer. When the elder Cook moved to the village of Ayton in 1736, his new employer recognized eight-year-old James as a bright youngster, and paid the fees to send him to the local school. A reasonably diligent student, James was said to have been good at his sums. He also helped around the farm where his father worked, until, at the age of 17, he obtained work as a clerk for a storekeeper in the nearby fishing village of Staithes. There the sea fastened its grip on him. After 18 months of keeping the accounts, he moved to the North Sea port of Whitby, where in July 1746 he signed indentures binding himself as an apprentice seaman for a coal shipper named John Walker.

Cook's first glimpse of seafaring life was from the decks of the *Freelove*, a 341-ton collier that regularly sailed from Whitby to London. The North Sea was a demanding school for the novice mariner. Crowded with sunken rocks and shifting sand shoals, subject to swift tidal currents and sudden storms, the waters off England's east coast are as treacherous as any in the world. In foul weather a grounded ship could be smashed to bits in minutes. Hundreds of Yorkshiremen lost their lives in North Sea squalls every year. Those who survived tended to be cautious and deliberate navigators.

When his term of apprenticeship was over in 1749, Cook remained with Walker's firm, serving on a second collier, the *Three Brothers*. By 1755, having studied astronomy and mathematics in his spare time and risen to the rank of mate, Cook was offered command of one of Walker's new ships. But life as a North Sea collier captain did not attract the 27-year-old mariner. He politely declined Walker's offer, informing his employer that he had "a mind to try his fortune" in the Royal Navy, and on June 17, 1755, he entered a Naval recruiting office near London and volunteered as an able seaman.

Ordered to Portsmouth, Cook was assigned to the 60-gun ship of the line *Eagle*. Most of the new recruits on the *Eagle* had no seafaring experience, and many of them had been rounded up by the Navy's notorious press gangs. It was obvious to the *Eagle's* captain, Joseph Hamar, that Cook was no ordinary recruit. Standing more than six feet tall, with piercing eyes and prominent eyebrows, Cook exuded an air of authority and performed every task just a bit better than expected.

With the outbreak of the Seven Years' War between England and France in 1756, the *Eagle* was assigned to blockade duty in the North Atlantic, and Cook learned the tough discipline of spending long months at sea. In 1758, having been promoted to the rank of master—in the 18th Century a warrant officer specializing in navigating and ship handling—Cook sailed the 64-gun *Pembroke* across the Atlantic and

H.M.S. "Endeavour": a doughty freighter adapted for discovery

H.M.S. *Endeavour* was not the Admiralty's first choice as the vessel to take James Cook's expedition to the Pacific in 1768. The Admiralty had settled on a 24-gun frigate when the Navy Board, a panel that supervised the Royal Navy's ships, pointed out that such a ship could not possibly carry enough food for so long a voyage. The board suggested "a cat-built vessel"—nautical jargon for a freighter with a deep waist and narrow stern. The Admiralty acquiesced, and within a week the board had purchased the collier *Earl of Pembroke*, which was soon renamed H.M.S. *Endeavour.*

The 366-ton vessel would never dazzle with her speed: She was shaped more like a shoe box than a sailing ship, with a bluff bow, slab sides and a small spread of sail. Her top speed was a mere eight knots, but she was small enough—106 feet long and 29 feet at the beam, drawing only 15 feet when fully loaded—to maneuver nimbly in reef-strewn waters. As Cook later observed, flat-bottomed colliers like the *Endeavour* could "safely sail near enough to land with time to turn away from warning sights, smells and sounds; if at the worst they took the ground, they could sit on it a while without much fear of a fatal capsize."

Moreover, the *Endeavour* proved to be superbly seaworthy in open waters. "The seamen say that they never knew a ship lay too so well as this does, so lively & at the same time so easy," noted one scientist. By the end of the voyage Cook had boundless faith in the converted collier, advising the Admiralty that in his opinion no other types of vessel "are proper to be sent on discoveries to distant parts."

H.M.S. ENDEAVOUR

To convert the *Endeavour* from a coastal collier run by a crew of about 15 to a survey vessel that could accommodate some 70 men for more than two years, Royal Navy shipwrights at the Deptford shipyard near London entirely rebuilt her interior, adding decks, cabins and storerooms wherever her basic structure permitted.

The poop was extended forward beyond the mainmast to provide headroom for new main-deck cabins in front of the 14-by-18-foot Great Cabin. A complete lower deck was built across the cavernous hold and partitioned at the stern into six tiny cabins for the ship's officers. At the bow, the new deck was fitted with cabins and storerooms for the carpenter and boatswain. In the bilges, new orlop decks created storerooms near the stern for the captain and steward, and in the bow for the gunner's magazine, with a platform to hold the gunpowder above the sloshing bilge water.

Even with all this renovation, the *Endeavour*'s accommodations were strained when her complement was expanded to 94 shortly before she sailed. Nearly 80 of the men slept wherever they could find space, either cheek-by-jowl in the forecastle—a low-ceilinged chamber they shared with spare hawsers—or on the stores that filled the lower deck. The only concession to comfort in the entire ship is not shown in these drawings, because Cook added it after the *Endeavour* left Deptford. It was a low platform over the tiller, built to allow genteel passengers to promenade on the poop without running afoul of the swinging tiller arm.

The vessel's four-year-old hull required no structural repairs, but it needed protection against the dreaded teredo, a wood-boring tropical sea worm that could devour whole planks in a matter of weeks. Shipwrights clad the *Endeavour* below the water line with an extra layer of half-inch deal planking closely covered with the large, flat heads of thousands of iron nails driven into the wood. The space between hull and sheathing was packed with a mucky compound of teredo deterrents: oakum, felt, horsehair, lime, linseed oil and tar.

The *Endeavour* was crammed with a veritable mountain of provisions: 17 tons of biscuit, 5 tons of flour, 2,500 pounds of raisins, 1,500 pounds of sugar, 500 gallons of vinegar, 1,200 gallons of beer and 1,600 gallons of brandy, among hundreds of other items. (To reveal the structure of the ship, most of the stores are omitted in this illustration.) Some space was conserved by substituting dismounted deck guns and galley coal for a portion of the usual iron ballast. Typically, Cook improved on even these measures on his next voyage to the Pacific. For that expedition, he said, the ship would be "so very full of Provisions & Stores that it will be impossible for me to allow a single Chest," so he took the unprecedented step of replacing his sailors' sea chests with specially made canvas duffel bags.

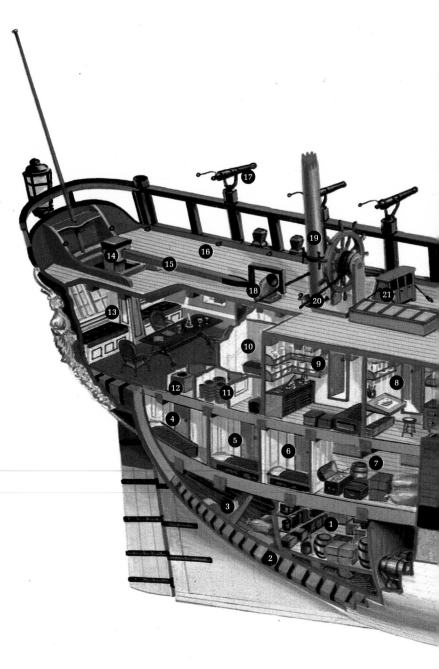

1. CAPTAIN'S STORES
2. FRAMES
3. KNEE
4. MASTER'S CABIN
5. SECOND LIEUTENANT'S CABIN
6. CLERK'S CABIN
7. LOWER DECK
8. DRAFTSMAN'S CABIN
9. ASTRONOMER'S CABIN
10. NATURALIST'S CABIN
11. CLOSETS
12. HEAD
13. GREAT CABIN
14. RUDDERHEAD
15. TILLER
16. POOP DECK
17. SWIVEL GUN
18. HEATING-STOVE CHIMNEY
19. MIZZENMAST
20. STEERING TACKLE
21. BINNACLE
22. BOLLARD
23. MAINMAST
24. COMPANIONWAY
25. SHIP'S PUMPS
26. CRUTCH
27. SIDE STEPS
28. FOUR-POUND GUN
29. MAIN HATCH
30. SPARE SPARS
31. LONGBOAT
32. FORE HATCH
33. WINDLASS
34. BELFRY
35. FOREMAST
36. CATHEAD
37. BOWSPRIT
38. GAMMON LASHING
39. STEM
40. VENTILATION PORT
41. FORECASTLE
42. SEA CHESTS
43. CARPENTER'S CABIN
44. CARPENTER'S WORKSHOP
45. SAIL LOCKER
46. WALE
47. POWDER MAGAZINE
48. HOLD
49. BALLAST
50. TEREDO DETERRENTS
51. DEAL PLANKING

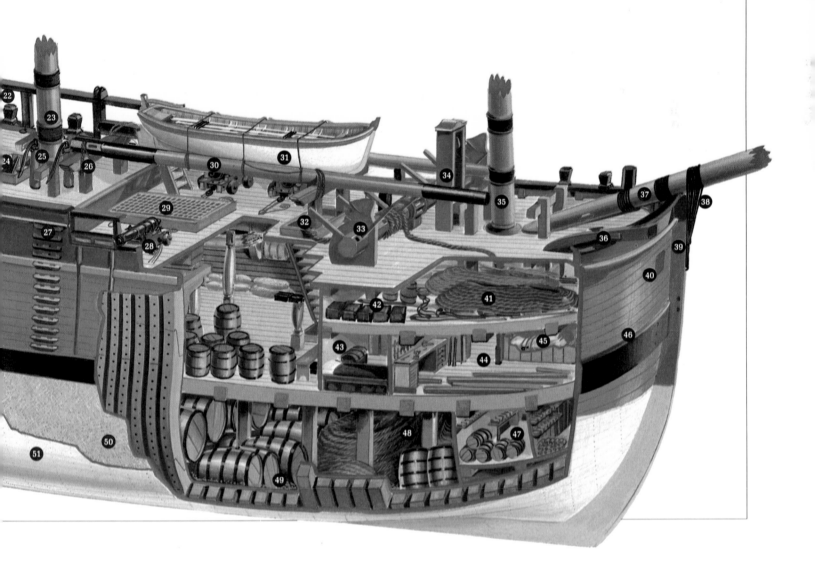

began the work that would bring him to the attention of the Navy's top command: the charting of the St. Lawrence River in preparation for the British assault on the French at Quebec. The French, anxious to deny the St. Lawrence to the British fleet, had removed all buoys from the shoal-filled river. Cook and a few other masters took soundings and relocated the channel, working mostly at night under threat of shore fire and Indian attacks. In the summer and fall of 1759, the British fleet ascended the St. Lawrence, and the French were outflanked and defeated.

For the remainder of the War, Cook perfected his new marine surveying skills, studying astronomy and Euclidian geometry, executing charts of the lower St. Lawrence, and compiling sailing directions for safe piloting into and out of many Canadian ports. Cook's charts already displayed the accuracy and attention to detail for which he later became famous. On January 19, 1761, Lord Colville, Commander in Chief of the North Atlantic Station, awarded Cook £50 for "his indefatigable Industry in making himself Master of the Pilotage of the River Saint Lawrence"—a sizable bonus for a master earning six guineas a month.

In 1762 Cook married and set up a home in the village of Mile End, near London. But he remained assigned to the North Atlantic Station, devoting his summers to a survey of the Newfoundland coastline and returning to England and his wife, Elizabeth, each winter. By now he was clearly marked for advancement. One superior officer informed the Admiralty that "from my Experience of Mr. Cook's Genius and Capacity, I think him well qualified for the Work he has performed, and for greater Undertakings of the same kind." Soon Cook was commanding his own surveying schooner, the *Grenville*, with a complement of 18 men.

At about this time an issue remote from the everyday concerns of pilotage began to shape Cook's destiny. It happened that the Royal Society of London, Britain's most distinguished scientific body, was planning an expedition to the Pacific to observe a rare astronomical event due to take place in June 1769. That month the orbit of Venus would cause the planet to pass across the face of the sun. From this event, known as the transit of Venus and not due to recur until 1874, astronomers hoped to obtain data that would help determine the earth's distance from the sun. Although the transit would be visible throughout the world, the Royal Society wanted to station observers at three widely separated locations: Hudson Bay, the North Cape of Norway and somewhere in the South Seas. Such separation would provide readings that could be checked against one another.

Upon learning that one of the locations would be somewhere in the South Pacific, an area of great political interest, the Crown contributed £4,000 to cover expenses and the Admiralty agreed to provide a ship. Not that the Navy was interested in astronomy, but the expedition might continue on and annex a few lands before the French got there—and perhaps even clear up the puzzle of the Southern continent.

The Royal Society's choice to command the expedition into the South Seas was Alexander Dalrymple, a highly talented, headstrong former functionary of the British East India Company. Dalrymple was England's foremost proponent of Terra Australis Incognita. A student of Pacific voyages, devotee of Quirós and an esteemed member of the Royal Soci-

Naturalist Joseph Banks, who went with Cook to the South Seas, donned a New Zealand Maori cloak for this portrait. Behind him are other souvenirs, including a feather headdress, an ornately carved war staff, and a canoe paddle. At his feet lie a Polynesian adz and a volume of plant drawings.

Daniel Solander, a Swedish botanist who volunteered to sail with Cook after learning of the expedition at a soiree in England, was esteemed for his character as well as his brilliance. "He is exceedingly sober, and very diligent," said one British scientist. "The more he is known, the more he is liked."

ety, he had examined scores of documents and ships' logs from past Pacific voyages, and from these records had written a book arguing the case for the existence of the great Southern land mass—and had even drawn a map outlining it. It was Dalrymple who had found the long-lost report of Luis Váez de Torres' passage through the strait between New Guinea and New Holland in 1606, forgotten for more than 150 years.

Hearing of the Royal Society's plans, Dalrymple had suggested himself as expedition leader, a proposal endorsed by the society's astronomical council. There was only one hitch. The Lords of the Admiralty stoutly insisted they would not entrust any royal ship to someone who was not a naval officer. Miffed, Dalrymple broke off discussions, refusing even to go along as an observer. The Admiralty then proposed the officer who, because of his special abilities, seemed uniquely fitted for the role: James Cook. The Royal Society, aware of Cook's accomplishments, approved the choice; when he came before the society's astronomical council, its members found that this stern-faced man spoke with conviction and was well versed in astronomy. The Navy promptly commissioned him a lieutenant and put him in charge of the *Endeavour*—a collier identical with those on which Cook had first gone to sea.

The 366-ton *Endeavour* would have to accommodate a party of 94. Cook was named the expedition's official astronomer. In this role he was to be assisted by Charles Green of the Royal Observatory at Greenwich. The position of resident naturalist went to Joseph Banks, a high-spirited, strapping, 25-year-old aristocrat who had conceived a zest for botany and zoology as a youngster and had distinguished himself as a natural scientist at Oxford. At his own expense he had journeyed to Newfoundland to observe flora and fauna. To friends who advised him to take the grand tour of Europe instead of joining Cook, Banks scoffed: "Every blockhead does that! My grand tour should be one round the world." His retinue included a second naturalist, Dr. Daniel Solander, who had studied with the famed Swedish botanist, Linnaeus, plus a secretary, two artists and four servants—all paid for out of Banks's pocket.

Stowing everybody and everything in the 106-foot *Endeavour* taxed even the unflappable Cook. "The gentlemen," as Banks, Solander and Green were called, each had a special cabin, bumping most of Cook's own officers to a lower deck. Banks and Solander also brought on board crate after crate of scientific equipment, including jars for specimens, pots, books, nets, canvases, easels, brushes and all manner of paraphernalia for catching and preserving insects. As official astronomer, Cook had requisitioned telescopes, quadrants, plane tables, micrometers, barometers and other instruments. The Royal Society added a portable observatory of wood and canvas, to be erected at the observation site.

The Admiralty victualed the *Endeavour* with enough salt meat and ship's biscuit to last 12 months. The supplies also included a number of special provisioning items to combat scurvy: 8,000 pounds of sauerkraut, 1,000 pounds of desiccated "portable soup," and large jars of "wort of malt" and "robs of oranges and lemons"—sugared syrups erroneously believed to be effective in treating advanced scurvy cases.

Amid the bustle of preparations, one important matter was settled. In late May, 1768, Captain Wallis had returned from his global circumnavi-

A journey that unlocked the secrets of New Zealand and Australia

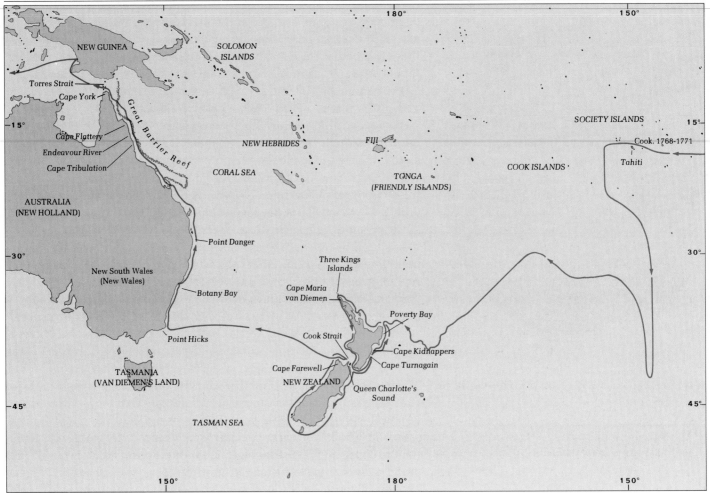

gation and reported his discovery of Tahiti; the Royal Society thereupon chose that island paradise as the site for the astronomical observation.

The *Endeavour* sailed from Plymouth on August 26, 1768. Within a few days the crew got notice of Cook's dietary zeal—and his strict discipline: Two men who refused to eat all their ration of fresh beef were given a dozen lashes each. Cook also ordered the men to wash regularly and keep their quarters clean, new habits to most of them. At Madeira he took on a load of fresh onions, which he issued to all hands.

Determined to educate his crew as he had taught himself, Cook set astronomer Green to work instructing the *Endeavour*'s midshipmen in shooting the sun. Cook also persuaded Green to teach the men the techniques for making lunar observations, the extremely complicated method that Bougainville's astronomer, Pierre Antoine Véron, had used for determining longitude. Though a British inventor had recently developed a chronometer that would revolutionize the art of longitude calculation (*page 147*), Cook did not have one. In any event, the lunar method proved as accurate in the hands of Green and Cook as it had in Véron's.

While still in the Atlantic, Cook endured his first trial of command. After crossing the Equator the *Endeavour* put in to Rio de Janeiro for

Entering the Pacific by way of Cape Horn, Cook brought the Endeavour to Tahiti in April 1769, and from there embarked on a looping track across the Southern latitudes. Upon reaching New Zealand, he circumnavigated both islands, then pressed on to the east coast of Australia. Heading north, Cook threaded the Great Barrier Reef, before sailing through the Torres Strait to the Indian Ocean, and thence home.

water and fresh provisions. Unfortunately, the Portuguese Viceroy refused to believe that the odd-looking *Endeavour* was an English Naval vessel; he suspected Cook and his men of being spies or smugglers, and threatened to jail anyone who disembarked. Banks and one of the artists, Sydney Parkinson, did manage to slip ashore one night to collect plants. Meanwhile, Cook carried on a furious paper war with the official for three weeks, drafting a series of indignant memorials with Banks's assistance. Eventually the Viceroy relented and supplied the English with food and water. "This morn, thank God we have got all we want from those illiterate impolite gentry," wrote Banks in his journal on December 2 as the *Endeavour* resumed her southward passage.

Morale was high on the 2,000-mile leg from Rio de Janeiro to Cape Horn. While Cook and Green continued to practice and refine their lunar observations, Banks and Solander busily took note of the natural phenomena. Sightings of petrels, albatrosses, sea turtles, seals and penguins were excitedly recorded in the naturalists' journals. During one calm spell the *Endeavour*'s rigging was covered with swarms of butterflies, and Banks gathered many of them up with the help of several crewmen, who were rewarded for their work with bottles of rum out of his own private stock. On Christmas Day, Cook permitted everyone to imbibe freely and, as Banks remembered, "All good Christians, that is to say all hands, got abominably drunk so that at night there was scarce a sober man in the ship. Wind, thank God, very moderate or the lord knows what would have become of us."

The weather became far less cooperative at the Strait of Le Maire, which Cook had decided to traverse en route to the Cape. Because of the biting cold, the crew were issued heavy woolen fearnought jackets and trousers. Now the *Endeavour* pitted herself against wicked Cape Horn snorters, and the stout little ship quickly proved herself equal to the challenge of the Southern ocean, although more than once Cook was forced to take in sail and lay to before the wind. "The *Endeavour*," wrote Banks, "has shown her excellence remarkably well, shipping scarce any water though it blew at times vastly strong."

Three times the ship was driven back from the entrance to the strait, her bowsprit pitching into the monstrous swells, before she finally worked up to a safe anchorage inside the Bay of Good Success (*page 116*). There Cook spent five days collecting green vegetables and water and studying the Fuegians, who survived on shellfish and eagerly accepted gifts of beads and glass. Once again Banks and Solander went botanizing, and Cook began to wonder at all the plants they were collecting, "most of them unknown in Europe and in that alone consisted their whole value." On one nature outing the temperature plummeted, snow fell and two of Banks's servants froze to death.

Leaving the strait, Cook headed southwest, reaching Cape Horn on January 27, 1769. To fix the location of the cape with absolute certainty, he sailed the *Endeavour* as close inshore as possible, meanwhile making several observations of the sun and moon. Later he wrote: "I can now venture to assert that the Longitude of few places in the World are better ascertained than that of Strait of Le Maire and Cape Horn."

Cook next decided to look for Terra Australis Incognita to the south-

west of Cape Horn. But when he reached lat. 60° 10′ S., long. 74° 30′ W., more than 600 miles from the Cape, there was no sign of land, only endless gigantic swells. In early February he altered course to the northwest, steering for Tahiti, and sailed over a large eastern chunk of the fabled continent as outlined by Dalrymple. Still he felt no land was near: "We have had no Current that hath affected the Ship Since we came into these Seas, this must be a great sign that we have been near no land of any extent because near land are generally found Currents." Even Banks, an avowed believer in the theoretical continent, marveled at "the number of square degrees of land which we have already changed into water."

Tropical birds were seen as the *Endeavour* skirted the coral-fringed Tuamotu atolls, discovered by Quirós in 1606. In early April Cook reached the latitude of Tahiti and, knowing he was somewhere east of the island, set his course directly westward (*map, page 114*). Tahiti was sighted on April 13, 1769, well ahead of schedule. All hands on the *Endeavour* were healthy. Two years previously, Wallis reached the island with 100 cases of scurvy aboard: Cook had none.

Cook anchored the *Endeavour* in Matavai Bay, a lovely crescent-shaped harbor protected from the open sea by a barrier reef. Because a

Islanders on Tierra del Fuego trade small amounts of food to Endeavour sailors for ribbons and glass beads. Other crewmen, protected by Marines, fill the ship's water casks in this painting by expedition artist Alexander Buchan.

lengthy stay in Tahiti was envisioned, Cook was determined that his relations with the Tahitians would be amicable but formal. The islanders soon put that resolution to the test.

The day after their arrival, Cook and his colleagues went ashore to be feted by two chiefs whom Banks—with the same classical bent that had motivated Bougainville in his impromptu name giving—dubbed Hercules and Lycurgus. While dining, Banks found himself seated beside a homely woman who was notably solicitous of his attention. He spied a "very pretty girl with a fire in her eyes," persuaded her to sit on the other side of him and was in the throes of extricating himself from the first woman when a cry went up from Dr. Solander and the surgeon, Dr. Monkhouse, that their pockets had been picked. Solander had lost his spyglass and Monkhouse his snuffbox. Banks leaped to his feet and slammed the butt of his gun down on the ground. This so alarmed the Tahitians that they fled from the tent. Only after considerable palaver were the objects retrieved and cordiality reestablished.

Cook had been warned before leaving England that the Tahitians might tax his patience, and he told his men to exercise "all imaginable humanity" in dealing with them. His forbearance paid off, for the few ugly incidents that did occur were smoothed over. Once some Marines assigned to protect the expedition shot and killed a local man caught attempting to steal a musket. Cook patiently explained to several of the victim's friends why his men had acted as they did, eventually managing to convince the Tahitians "that we would still be friends with them."

Cook entrusted Banks and Solander with the responsibility of bartering for food—a wise move, since Banks was both scrupulously fair and alert to the subtleties of the Polynesians' culture. The naturalist became an enthusiast of everything Tahitian, not just the island's plants, birds and insects but its social customs as well. At one point he had himself

Huddling around a fire in a conical hut, a local family takes shelter from the extreme cold of Tierra del Fuego. Cook sympathetically described the inhabitants of the island as "perhaps as miserable a set of People as are this day upon Earth."

copiously daubed with charcoal and joined a ceremonial procession that wound along the shore. No blockhead on the European grand tour could have experienced anything like that.

Meanwhile, the Englishmen began to prepare for their observation of the transit of Venus, which was to occur on June 3. Cook named the northernmost tip of Matavai Bay Point Venus and ordered the construction of a small fort there to protect the scientific equipment. Surrounded by earthworks and palisades and armed with six swivel guns, the encampment was guarded around the clock and called Fort Venus.

Despite all these precautions, an irreplaceable quadrant was stolen the morning after the English carried it ashore. "It had never been taken out of the packing case," fumed Cook, who quickly ordered the whole bay sealed off and all canoes seized until the instrument, essential for the observation, was returned. Banks and astronomer Green set off on foot in pursuit of a suspect identified by one of the chiefs. They covered almost seven miles before catching up with a group of Tahitians who, according to the informant, were accomplices. After lengthy discussions, the missing device was produced, but the thief was never found.

On the day of the transit, June 3, the skies were clear (and the temperature 119° F.). Cook, Green and Solander each manned a telescope at Fort Venus during the six-hour period of transit. Perplexingly, their timings of the transit were slightly different. It turned out that similar discrepancies had occurred at all the observation stations around the world—the product of a complex optical phenomenon. In consequence, the astronomers of the Royal Society failed to accomplish their goal of accurately computing the sun's distance from the earth.

Although he had completed his astronomical assignment, Cook did not leave Tahiti immediately. First, the *Endeavour* had to be scraped, calked and repainted, a job that took longer than expected because the men were spending inordinate amounts of time ashore with female companions. Second, Cook wanted to chart the coastline of Tahiti, and so he and Banks set off in a pinnace on a six-day circumnavigation of the island. At one point they stopped in a bay where, said the local Tahitians, foreign ships had come the year before; Cook conjectured that the visitors had been Spanish. They had, in fact, been French members of Bougainville's expedition. The Englishmen continued along the shore, meeting a succession of chieftains, inspecting shrines and sketching the coastline. The resulting chart *(page 120)*, Cook reported in his journal, "cannot be very accurate." He was being excessively modest; later visitors to Tahiti found Cook's chart amazingly precise.

Soon after Cook and Banks returned to Matavai Bay, the *Endeavour* was ready to leave. At the last moment two Marines decamped to the mountains with island girls. Cook had heard there had been talk of mutiny, and he moved swiftly to recapture the men. He rounded up all the chiefs he could find—half a dozen—and said they would be held hostage until someone revealed where the men had taken refuge. Within hours the Tahitians managed to locate the two Marines and hustle them aboard the *Endeavour*.

On July 13, Cook bid the islanders farewell, noting that "several of them were in tears" as the crew loosed all sail. Aboard ship were two

As sketched by Cook, the Union Jack waves over Fort Venus, an astronomical observation post he built on Tahiti to time the transit of Venus across the face of the sun—and thus help determine the distance of the sun from the earth. The scientific instruments were housed in tentlike structures brought from England.

additions to the company: a local priest named Tupaia, who was skilled in Polynesian techniques of navigation, and his servant boy. Banks offered to support Tupaia in England, writing in his journal: "Thank heaven I have a sufficiency and I do not know why I may not keep him as a curiosity, as well as some of my neighbors do lions and tygers."

Cook was now following secret orders handed to him by the Admiralty at the outset of the voyage. They directed him to sail the *Endeavour* as far south as 40° to search for Terra Australis Incognita, whose discovery would "redound greatly to the honour of this nation as a maritime power, as well as to the dignity of the Crown of Great Britain, and the advancement of the trade and navigation thereof." If Cook sighted the continent, he was to explore its coastline and establish friendly relations with its inhabitants. But, continued the orders, "not having discovered it, you are to proceed to the westward, between latitude 40° and 35° until reaching the eastern coast of New Zealand, and explore as great an extent of the coast as you can."

With Tupaia to guide him, Cook first visited some of Tahiti's neighboring isles, naming the group the Society Islands, "as they lay contiguous to one another." Then the *Endeavour*, Banks wrote, "launched out into the Ocean in search of what chance or Tupaia might direct us to." As the ship bore southward, the officers and the gentlemen began to take sides for or against the existence of the continent. Cook declared himself open-minded, although he was skeptical of the evidence presented by Dalrymple and other theorists.

One day he altered course to investigate a dark shape that looked like land on the eastern horizon, but it turned out to be "only clouds." Bearing southward once again, the *Endeavour* encountered no continent, but plenty of hail squalls and cold weather. On August 26, 1769, the anniversary of their departure from England, Cheshire cheese and porter were served in the Great Cabin, whose occupants for the moment, said Banks, "liv'd like English men." The 40° parallel was crossed on September 1, with no hint of land ahead, and because the weather was "so very Tempestuous" Cook reluctantly gave up the search and veered to the northwest, "lest we should receive such damages in our sails and rigging as might hinder the further prosecutions of the voyage." After a few days he bore to the west, in accordance with his instructions. He promised a gallon of rum to the first person who sighted land.

"Our old enemy Cape fly away entertained us," reported Banks on October 5, as another cloud bank deceived the sailors. But at 2 p.m. two days later, the rum was won by Nicholas Young, a 12-year-old boy who had been on watch at the ship's masthead. The boy was subsequently

Coral reefs ring the volcanic island of Tahiti and its smaller neighbor Eimeo—now called Moorea—in this chart compiled by James Cook. The place names are Cook's literations of local names for villages and natural features, and the numbers dotting the waters of Tahiti are his depth soundings, given in fathoms.

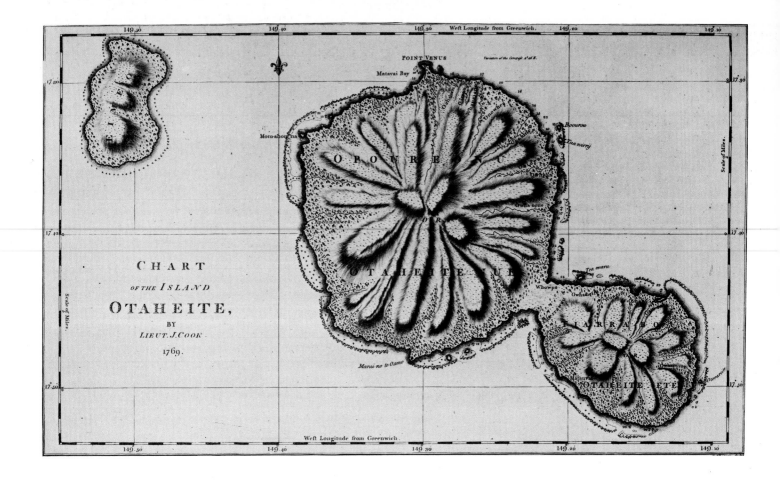

A friendly Maori tribesman offers a lobster to a sailor in exchange for a piece of white cloth, in this watercolor by an anonymous Endeavour crewman. New Zealand lobsters weighed an average of 11 pounds, and naturalist Joseph Banks pronounced them "certainly the largest and best I have ever eaten."

given another honor; Cook named a promontory near the landfall for him: Young Nick's Head. The Endeavour had reached the east coast of the north island of New Zealand, not seen by Europeans since Tasman's visit 127 years earlier. The next night Banks excitedly declared that the landfall was "certainly the continent we are in search of." Cook was not sure, although he admitted that "the land is high with white steep cliffs and back inland are very high mountains." Whether it was continent or island, Cook was determined to examine the land mass closely.

The first two days were inauspicious. Putting into a bay from whose beaches smoke was seen rising, Cook went ashore and found the inhabitants hostile. When they threatened to seize the pinnace, his men opened fire with their muskets, killing one man. The next day Cook and his party tried to intercept a canoe to talk with its occupants; fighting broke out again, and the English guns claimed three more lives. Finally Cook was able to arrange a parley, and Tupaia found that the inhabitants understood his inquiries perfectly, identifying themselves as Maoris. They were a Polynesian people who shared a common ancestry with the Tahitians, but—as Tasman had learned—were often exceedingly warlike.

Cook was anguished over using force against the brave but uncomprehending Maoris, even in self-defense: "I can by no means justify my conduct in attacking and killing the people in this boat who had given me no just provocation," he wrote. Echoed Banks: "Thus ended the most disagreeable day My life has yet seen, black be the mark for it."

Unable to obtain food or water, Cook pulled out of the harbor, which he named Poverty Bay "because it afforded us no one thing we wanted," and began coasting southward, sounding depths and charting the shoreline. He continued to run afoul of the Maoris: In one bay they almost made off with Tupaia's boy, prompting Cook to name a nearby headland Cape Kidnappers. Reaching lat. 40° S. and finding no likely anchorages, Cook reversed course. He designated a nearby point Cape Turnagain, a label that, like many he conferred, would last to modern times.

North of Poverty Bay, the coast was more attractive and the people friendlier. At one inlet a shore party was able to collect wood, water and two sorts of edible greens: wild celery and "scurvy grass," a type of cress. At another point Maoris paddled canoes out to the Endeavour to trade fish, sweet potatoes and other foodstuffs for iron spikes, beads and pieces of Tahitian cloth. On October 23 the Endeavour anchored in a little cove with a fine sandy bottom. Cook went ashore, climbed a hill and found the countryside cultivated and handsome. Banks and Solander botanized freely, the artists sketched Maori canoes, and the crew of the Endeavour worked to repair the ship's steering gear, which had been weakened by the strong gales of the previous weeks.

Leaving six days later, the English proceeded northward by easy stages, trading with the Maoris when possible. As always, Cook mapped the coastline with meticulous care—a formidable task when undertaken from a moving ship at varying distances from the shore—and baptized promontories and bays with inexhaustible imagination.

On November 4, Cook stopped for 11 days to make a second astronomical observation—the transit of Mercury across the sun—and named the spot Mercury Bay. Less than 50 miles farther on he pronounced a large river the Thames and noted that the shore nearby was a likely spot for settlement (years later the city of Auckland flourished there). After the Englishmen were forced to fire their guns to scare off threatening Maoris in a fleet of canoes, he named a point in the vicinity Cape Runaway. In a lighter mood, the expedition dubbed one group of islands the Court of Aldermen, after the City of London's governing body, and—wrote Banks—"entertained ourselves some time with giving names to each of them from their resemblance, thick and squat or lank and tall, to some one or other of those respectable citizens."

Some of the Maoris Cook met were awe-struck by the newcomers. Decades later one aged chief vividly recalled the day in his childhood when the *Endeavour* anchored near his village. The Englishmen were thought to be supernatural people with eyes in the backs of their skulls, because they rowed their boats facing the sterns. One man, he remembered, collected shells and flowers. Another, very tall, was clearly the lord: He seldom spoke but was interested in everything about him, and patted the children's cheeks and gently touched their heads.

By the second week of December, Cook was near New Zealand's northern tip. On the 13th the weather turned stormy and the wind howled in from the northwest—exactly the direction in which Cook was headed.

In a sketch by Cook, sentinels stand watch at a picket-fortified Maori stronghold perched on a natural rock arch on the coast of New Zealand. Cook wrote that "the best Engineer in Europe" could not have chosen a better defensive placement. "It is strong by Nature and made more so by Art."

Clad in a flax cape, an elaborately tattooed Maori displays his long pendant earring, comb, feathers and necklace in this portrait by Endeavour artist Sydney Parkinson. Cook was fascinated by the patterns of the New Zealanders' tattoos: "They are so exact in the application of these Figures," he observed, "that no difference can be found between the one side of the face and the other."

The *Endeavour*, sailing under double-reefed topsails, was blown off the coast. Slowly Cook beat back. In heavy seas he rounded a cape that he rightly deduced was "the northern extremity of this country."

The winds abated on the expedition's second Christmas, and all hands, wrote Banks, feasted on "goose pie made from gannets" and got uproariously drunk "as our forefathers used to be upon the like occasion." Then the weather worsened again, and Cook had to stand out to sea to avoid being driven onto the rocky shore. On New Year's Day, 1770, he stood on the *Endeavour's* lurching deck and calmly fixed the position of Cape Maria van Diemen on the northwest corner of the island to within two minutes of its true latitude and four minutes of its true longitude. That evening he noted in his journal that the "gale of wind for its strength and continuance was such as I hardly was ever in before."

He desperately needed to overhaul the *Endeavour*; her bottom was foul and her seams had to be recalked. But the west coast of New Zealand was desolate and he continued to head south. By January 14, the land's features were more promising and Cook anchored in a "very broad and deep Bay." It was, as he suspected, the same body of water in which Tasman's Murderer's Bay was located. Cook sailed across the immense sound for two days before entering a long inlet near its southeastern corner and anchoring the *Endeavour* in a "very snug cove."

The inlet, which he "dignified with the name of Queen Charlotte's Sound," was an ideal spot to careen the *Endeavour* and replenish supplies. There were abundant fresh water, lush forests and a multitude of tasty fish: "Having the seine net with us," wrote Cook, "we made a few hauls and caught 300 pound of different sorts of fish." The local Maoris were less truculent than those who had savaged Tasman's men at Murderer's Bay. Approaching the little cove where the *Endeavour* was anchored, they heaved a few stones at the ship. But they became hospitable once Tupaia convinced them that the English meant no harm.

The overhaul of the *Endeavour* commenced the following day. While the sailors careened the ship and began to scrub her hull, Cook, Banks and the other gentlemen went ashore, where they discovered that the inhabitants of Queen Charlotte's Sound were cannibals. "A few days ago," wrote Cook, "they had taken, killed and eaten a boat's crew of their enemies." But the Maoris made no move against the Englishmen; instead, they traded cheerfully for iron nails and pieces of cloth.

An infinitely more important discovery soon followed. On January 22, Cook set out in the pinnace "with a view to examine the head of the inlet" and to discover the limits of the broad bay he had crossed. The next day, after climbing a steep hill, he found the view open to the east. There, to his delight, "I saw what I took to be the Eastern Sea and a strait or passage from it into the Western Sea." So New Zealand was two bodies of land, not one, and Queen Charlotte's Sound, where the *Endeavour* was anchored, lay on the northern tip of the south island. Modestly, Cook did not mention in his journal the name given to the passage. Evidently it was Banks who insisted that for once the leader's name be used: The passage became Cook Strait.

Having calked and reprovisioned the *Endeavour* and taken possession of Queen Charlotte's Sound "and adjacent lands"—a ceremony he had already performed on the northern island—Cook set sail on February 5 and passed through his strait, carefully noting its treacherous tides. His object now was to find out how big the southern island was. A few officers, however, were still not convinced that the land on the north side of the strait was insular: Perhaps it was a peninsula of Terra Australis Incognita. "To clear up every doubt that might arise," Cook plied up the eastern coast to Cape Turnagain. Sighting it, he called the officers on deck, and all agreed that his conclusions about geography were right.

Now Cook turned and headed southwest. Again speculation arose: Was the southern land perhaps part of the continent they were seeking? By March 13 the *Endeavour* had rounded what was unquestionably the southern tip of New Zealand's south island. The Terra Australis proponents were chagrined. "Blew fresh all day," noted Banks, "but carried us round the Point to the total demolition of our aerial fabrick called continent." Cook coasted up the south island's forbidding western shore without stopping until late March, when the *Endeavour* arrived back in Cook Strait and anchored in an inlet that he called Admiralty Bay.

Cook had now fulfilled all his instructions—magnificently. He had sailed where the Admiralty had directed him, investigated all signs of land and found no continent. He had circumnavigated both of New Zealand's large islands, minutely charting some 2,400 miles of coastline and collecting a vast amount of information. After a few early skirmishes he had gotten along well with the Maoris. Banks and Solander had acquired 400 new plants. Already Cook's voyage aboard the *Endeavour* had accomplished more systematic discovery than that of any previous Pacific navigator. It was time to sail home. But by what route? Cook's instructions left the decision to him.

He put the alternatives to his officers. They could sail east in high latitudes to Cape Horn; this should settle once and for all the continental question. But the Southern winter was approaching, and Cook did not think the *Endeavour*, after all she had been through, was strong enough to withstand the beating she would take off Cape Horn. They could head west through the same stormy latitudes for the Cape of Good Hope, but this course also would be overly taxing for the ship. They could make for the East Indies, going north around the eastern tip of New Guinea as Tasman had done; yet somehow this prospect did not seem challenging.

There was one additional possibility, and Cook favored it: to sail for the still-undiscovered east coast of New Holland—present-day Australia—and upon meeting those shores to steer north and seek the Torres Strait between New Holland and New Guinea, which Cook knew about from Dalrymple's book. The prospect of exploring yet another unknown land was simply too exciting to pass up. The decision was unanimous: They would head for New Holland. It was a classic demonstration of Cook's penchant for boldly exceeding what was expected of him.

Cook named the last visible headland of New Zealand Cape Farewell and then shaped a westerly course that would take the *Endeavour* to the northernmost point Tasman had reached on Van Diemen's Land in 1642. From this spot Cook planned to venture toward the east coast of New Holland, which he knew lay somewhere farther north. However, a southerly gale blew the *Endeavour* more than 150 miles off course. As a result,

Maori fishermen on New Zealand's Queen Charlotte's Sound haul in their catch in basket-like nets woven from a broad-bladed grass. The nets, wrote Cook, were "very ingeniously made; in the middle of these they tie the bait, then sink the Nett to the bottom with a stone; after it lays there a little time they haul it Gently up, and hardly ever without fish."

Maori warriors in a large canoe try to frighten the Englishmen on the Endeavour by sticking out their tongues and chanting taunts. The New Zealanders dropped their aggressive posture after the Endeavour's guns were fired, throwing stone balls—wrote Cook— "farther than they could comprehend."

when Lieutenant Zachary Hicks saw land at 6 a.m. on April 19, it was the southeastern corner of Australia, not Van Diemen's Land.

Cook named the landfall Point Hicks, started a new series of charts and began sailing up the coast. After a while the extent of the shoreline made him realize that he was off the east coast of New Holland. Smoke rose here and there, and the countryside seemed agreeable, although sparsely vegetated and rocky. Banks said that it resembled "the back of a lean Cow, covered in general with long hair, but nevertheless where her scraggy hip bones have stuck out farther than they ought accidental rubs and knocks have entirely bared them of their share of covering."

For several days Cook could find no spot to put in, "as we had a large hollow sea from the SE rowling in which beat everywhere high upon the shore." But on April 29 a large sheltered bay was found. A few aborigines threw some spears without hitting anyone as the *Endeavour*'s landing party approached, then ran away. Just before stepping ashore, Cook turned to Midshipman Isaac Smith, who was his wife's cousin, and said, "Isaac, you shall land first," whereupon young Smith became the first European to set foot on Australia's east coast.

Cook stayed at the anchorage for nine days, surveying the "safe and commodious" harbor, and Banks and Solander obtained scores of new plant specimens in the verdant countryside. So excited were they over the new-found flora that Cook, who had decided to call the place Stingray Harbor, changed his appellation to Botanist Harbor, and finally to Botany Bay. As the *Endeavour* crept northward, keeping two to three miles off the low-lying coast, Cook stationed men at the bow to take soundings, and from time to time he sent a boat ahead to examine the shoals and breakers, which could be seen both inshore and far out to sea. By mid-May the number of obstructions was increasing—a trend noted in names like Point Danger, Mount Warning and Cape Tribulation.

On May 28 the *Endeavour* survived a close call at a spot where the seabed suddenly thrust up from 17 fathoms to three fathoms; Cook was forced to "immediately let go an anchor and brought the ship up with all sails standing." Requiring more fresh water, he put into a bay, but "not one drop could be found"; annoyed, he called the place Thirsty Sound.

As the coastline led northwest, the passages between the shoals narrowed. Unknowingly, Cook had sailed inside the Great Barrier Reef, the 1,200-mile collection of jagged coral structures that guards the northeast coast of Australia. Cook picked his way through the coral outcroppings. On June 10 he noticed that the soundings were varying widely. But at 10 p.m. the *Endeavour* was in 21 fathoms (more than 125 feet), and the captain felt safe in going to bed. Shortly thereafter there was a great grinding noise. The ship had struck on the reef, and it was high tide.

Cook was on deck in a moment, coolly giving orders. Boats carried the anchors out and dropped them for heaving off, but the *Endeavour* would not budge. Everything heavy that could be spared was jettisoned: casks, old stores, ballast, finally six of the guns and their carriages. Yards and topmasts were struck and floated in the water alongside—still with no results. The tide ebbed, and the ship heeled only slightly. Cook was more grateful than ever for the *Endeavour*'s flat bottom: A deep-draft warship with a V-shaped bottom would have toppled onto her side.

When the tide rose at daybreak, the *Endeavour* remained stuck. And now she was leaking seriously. Everyone, scientists included, manned the pumps. Banks later remarked on the quiet assurance of the officers and the cheerfulness of the crew, but there was no mistaking their peril. "This was an alarming and I may say terrible circumstance," said Cook, "and threatened immediate destruction to us." Just as the predicament seemed hopeless, someone recalled that the tides along the coast had been higher at night. Buoyed by this thought, the men pumped still harder, barely keeping up with the water pouring into the bilge.

As darkness fell, Cook decided to make his move. At 10 p.m., 23 hours after running aground, all hands went to the capstan. They pushed for all their might, and as the anchor line reeled in inch by inch the *Endeavour* slipped off the reef and floated. Anchors and spars were brought back on board, sail was made and, with four feet of water in her hold, the ship edged in for the mainland and urgent repairs.

A midshipman named Jonathan Monkhouse suggested they slow the leak from the outside of the hull by a process called fothering. He had seen it done once. Cook assented and put Monkhouse in charge of the operation. A spare sail sewed with tufts of wool and oakum and covered with dense, sticky sheep dung was lowered over the *Endeavour's* bow and dragged into position over the hole, where it was held in place by the pressure of the water. The effect was almost instantaneous: The leak slowed to a trickle. A party sent ahead to look for a harbor located a small river where the ship could be beached, and after Cook personally marked the channel into the river's mouth the *Endeavour* limped in and anchored. Inspection of her bottom showed how lucky Cook and his men had been: As the ship was being kedged off the reef, a piece of coral as big as a man's fist had lodged in the hole, helping to stanch the leak.

The ship was to spend almost two months in the Endeavour River, as Cook named the desolate inlet; although the patching was completed by July 4, a steady southeast wind pinned the men in their refuge. The naturalists gathered more plants; Cook and Green made observations of Jupiter's moons; crewmen found cockles that contained 20 pounds of meat each, and a large, odd-looking, long-tailed animal that hopped prodigiously was shot by one of the ship's officers, Lieutenant John Gore. "I should have taken it for a wild dog but for its running in which it jumped like a hare or deer," wrote Cook. Banks later recorded that the region's inhabitants called it a "kangaru."

The aborigines kept their distance for a full month before deciding to risk a parley. "They were wholly naked, their skins the color of wood soot or a dark chocolate," Cook commented after the encounter. The sailors called the bones the people had in their noses "spritsail yards." But the Englishmen did not think it funny when the aborigines, angered at not being given a share of some turtles caught by the crew, set fire to the dry grass around the encampment, destroying some of the supplies.

A worse threat lay offshore. One day Cook climbed a hill and looked out over the reef area. "I saw what gave me no small uneasiness," he wrote, "which were a number of sand banks or shoals laying all along the coast." He had to find a way out to the north or northeast, for the prevailing wind prevented any retreat to the south. On August 6 the wind briefly shifted. With the pinnace ahead taking soundings and Cook at the masthead for the best possible view, the *Endeavour* sailed out. There were breakers everywhere, and progress was agonizingly slow. At one point he thought he saw a clear passage, only to find the way blocked by coral. He indignantly named the nearby headland Cape Flattery. Finally, on August 12, Cook and Banks landed on a small island, climbed to its highest point and glimpsed an escape route. The next day the *Endeavour* sailed into the open sea.

But freedom had a price. Cook was now too far from the coast to continue charting it. Furthermore, by sailing outside the Barrier Reef, he might miss the Torres Strait, which he felt must be not far distant. So, despite the ordeals of the coral maze, he resolved "to get in with the land as soon as I can do it with safety."

Two days later the *Endeavour* had edged to within a mile of the reef. Tremendous breakers hurled themselves against the jagged coral, sending up geysers of water and foam. As Cook sought an opening, the wind suddenly died. To the crew's horror, the ground swell kept carrying them closer to the surf. The leadsman paid out his entire 140-fathom line and found no bottom: The reef was a perpendicular coral wall rising straight out of the depths. So there could be no anchoring to halt the *Endeavour*'s progress toward destruction.

Cook ordered the boats out to try to tow the ship to safety. The oarsmen strained at their sweeps, but the *Endeavour* continued to drift toward the coral. The distance to the breakers narrowed to 100 yards, then 80. "Now was our case truly desperate," recalled Banks. "A speedy death was all we had to hope for. That the vastness of the Breakers must quickly dash the ship to pieces was scarce to be doubted."

At the last moment the merest whiff of air—a cat's-paw—strayed in their direction. The *Endeavour* caught it and moved slightly away from the reef. The wind died, then revived, and the ship was blown a few yards farther from the surf. Cook saw a small gap in the reef and directed the oarsmen to pull for it. The ship slowly drew abreast of the break in the coral, only to be swept a quarter of a mile out to sea by an ebb tide rushing from the opening. Now Cook spotted another narrow gap. Again the oarsmen pulled. By the time the ship reached the opening, the tide had turned, and the *Endeavour* was swept inside the Barrier Reef once more. Cook anchored in smooth water.

It had been "the narrowest Escape we ever had," wrote one of the crew, "and had it not been for the immediate help of Providence we must Inevitably have perished." Cook named the passage Providential Channel, confessing in his journal, "it is but a few days ago that I rejoicd at having got without the Reef, but that joy was nothing when Compared to what I now felt at being safe at an Anchor within it."

In order to justify the enormous risks he had taken, Cook felt compelled to write: "People will hardly admit of an excuse for a man leaving a coast unexplored he has once discovered. I must own that I have engaged more among the Islands and Shoals upon this Coast than Perhaps in prudence I ought to have done with a single Ship, and every other thing considerd. But if I had not I should not have been able to give any better account of the one half of it, than if I had never seen it.''

He pressed on, with two boats reconnoitering ahead. The going was tortuous, and some days the *Endeavour* made only a few miles. Cook, who designated the entire area LABYRINTH on his chart, noted that ''so much does great danger swallow up lesser ones that those once so dreaded shoals were now looked at with less concern.''

On August 21, after five harrowing days inside the reef, Cook saw that the coastline of New Holland was curving westward; soon the *Endeavour* was riding a strong tidal current through a passage just beyond the mainland's northernmost tip. She was in part of the Torres Strait. Cook named the mainland promontory Cape York; his particular passage—

An exploring party leaves the camp where Cook spent seven weeks after his ship struck the Great Barrier Reef in June 1770. While carpenters patched the Endeavour's hull, the scientists made coastal trips by boat to observe such Australian oddities as anthills six feet high and 300-pound sea turtles.

slightly south of the route Torres had taken—came to be called Endeavour Strait. Cook, Banks and Solander rowed to a small island, climbed a hill and saw open water leading to the west: the Indian Ocean. Cook formally took possession of the entire eastern coastal area of New Holland; he named it New Wales—later amended to New South Wales.

Entering the Indian Ocean, Cook bore northwest for New Guinea, landed briefly on its south shore and then headed for the Dutch East Indies. Full of good cheer, the company sailed into Batavia on October 10, 1770. Almost everyone on board was healthy; in more than two years only four or five seamen had come down with scurvy, and all those had recovered—a signal accomplishment. When a boatload of Dutch offi-

cials came alongside to inspect the newcomer, the *Endeavour's* robust crew jeered at them for their pallid faces.

The jeering was premature, for at Batavia came a tragic denouement to the otherwise triumphant voyage. No one who visited the swampy, fetid city was immune to its pestilences. Had Cook been able to limit his stay to a few days, no great harm would have come to his men. But the *Endeavour* was found to be in need of major repairs. Her planking had been so worn down by the coral that it was only an eighth of an inch thick in spots, and many of her severely worm-eaten timbers had to be replaced. The repairs took four weeks, and by the time the ship was fit for sea again most of the crew were sick.

The chief enemy was malaria. It claimed the surgeon, Dr. Monkhouse, then Tupaia and his servant boy and four others. Banks and Solander were also stricken, but they survived. When Cook was finally ready to sail on December 26, only half his crew were available to work the ship, so he took on 19 new men from Batavia. As soon as the *Endeavour* got to sea, another scourge, dysentery, struck the sailors, and in the next six weeks 23 more died, including the astronomer Green, the artist Parkinson, the sailmaker, the cook and the carpenter.

Cook too had fallen ill, although—true to character—he did not mention it in his journal. As the *Endeavour* crossed the Indian Ocean he recorded the deaths laconically, sometimes adding a brief tribute. One entry in his log noted "the calamitous situation we are at present in, having hardly well men enough to tend the sails and look after the sick."

The *Endeavour* stopped at Capetown on March 15, 1771. Fortunately the air in this port was salubrious, and all but four of the company recovered fully during the ship's stay of a month. There were to be only two more deaths, those of Master Robert Molyneux on April 15 and Lieutenant Hicks on May 25. Hicks had been suffering from tuberculosis during the entire voyage and died in the mid-Atlantic. One notable survivor was the ship's goat, which had been carried all this way for the purpose of supplying milk for the officers' coffee; she had previously accompanied Wallis on his voyage, and now had the distinction of being the only goat to have made two circumnavigations of the globe.

On July 10, 1771, Nicholas Young, the same Young Nick who had first sighted New Zealand, called out the sighting of Land's End, and three days later Cook anchored in the Downs and was off to London to report to the Admiralty. He had been away almost three years.

He had sent from Batavia a preliminary report of the main events of the expedition. In it he played down his achievement. "Although the discoveries made in this voyage are not great," he wrote, "I flatter myself that they are such as may merit the attention of their Lordships, and altho' I have fail'd in discovering the so much talk'd of southern continent (which perhaps does not exist), yet I am confident that no part of the failure of such discovery can be laid to my charge. Had we been so fortunate not to have run ashore, much more would have been done in the latter part of the voyage than what was, but as it is I presume this voyage will be found as compleat as any before made to the South Seas."

Not only was it complete, it was the most productive expedition ever sent to the Pacific. From the standpoint of diet and disease prevention

An Australian kangaroo, painted by an artist in England from skins collected by Cook's expedition, stands on its long, powerful hind legs, poised to hop. Naturalist Joseph Banks was amazed when an 80-pound kangaroo easily eluded one of the ship's greyhounds.

alone, Cook's performance—up to Batavia—was unmatched. Yet he won no hero's status. The Lords of the Admiralty, after gulping at his extensive journal, stated their approval of his conduct, and in due course promoted him one step up to commander. He had a brief audience with King George III, who pronounced himself pleased at what the explorer had done. The public, for its part, hardly seemed aware of Cook. All the glory was focused on Banks and Solander, who were lionized by the English press as if the voyage had been theirs alone. They had come back, said one admirer, "laden with the greatest treasure of natural history that ever was brought into any country at one time by two persons."

The Royal Society achieved the finest touch of irony. They expressed gratitude to Cook for not using up the royal grant of £4,000 that had been awarded to cover costs of the celestial observation in Tahiti, and they generously voted to use the extra money to pay for a bust—not of Cook but of their monarch.

Cook did not seem to mind being ignored and did not invite inquiry. He preferred to spend the time with his wife and young children on the outskirts of London, and his mind was already busy on a matter more important than fame: He was making plans for a second Pacific voyage.

A hard-working artist's brilliant legacy

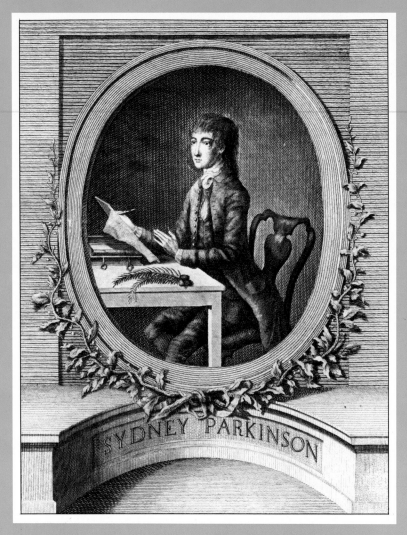

Sydney Parkinson is portrayed as a frail young man in an engraving from his Journal of a Voyage to the South Seas, *an account of his experiences that was published posthumously in 1773 by his brother, Stanfield.*

Sydney Parkinson boasted few scientific credentials in 1768, when, at the age of 23, he embarked on the *Endeavour* as a botanical draftsman. The son of a bankrupt Edinburgh brewer, Parkinson had spent several years as a disgruntled apprentice to a woolen draper before taking up a career in still-life drawing. In 1767 he was introduced to naturalist Joseph Banks who, after examining the young artist's finely rendered sketches of fruits and flowers, offered him £80 a year to accompany Cook's expedition to the South Seas.

Intelligent and keenly observant, Parkinson quickly became an indispensable member of the expedition's scientific party. He worked every day in the *Endeavour's* Great Cabin, sketching new plant specimens for Banks's rapidly expanding botanical collection. Each drawing was a careful record of a plant's shape, size, coloration, foliage and fruit. Afterward the naturalists dried the specimens on unbound sheets of John Milton's *Paradise Lost* that they had obtained at a cut-rate price from an overambitious London printer.

Many of Parkinson's sketches were produced under exceedingly trying circumstances. As collecting parties assembled piles of newly killed fish and birds, he sometimes found himself in a race with nature, hurrying to record the features of the specimens before they decomposed in the tropical heat. On one occasion, swarms of flies not only covered his subject, but ate the pigments off Parkinson's drawing paper as fast as his brush strokes could be applied.

Like other members of Cook's expedition, Parkinson completed a will before leaving England, fatalistically acknowledging that, "God knows I may never return." He never did. When the *Endeavour* reached the South Atlantic on the homeward run, he contracted dysentery and died within a few days. Banks returned to England with Parkinson's matchless collection of some 1,300 paintings and sketches, which he intended to publish in one grand volume. Unfortunately, the irrepressible naturalist—showing the same sort of "unbounded industry" that he had admired in the young artist—pursued so many new botanizing projects that he never found the time to complete the great opus. In consequence, Parkinson's talent went largely unrecognized until the publication of the bulk of his works more than two centuries later.

Clusters of four-pound fruits grew on the 40-foot-high, glossy-leaved breadfruit tree, called uru by the Tahitians and labeled Sitodium altile by the Endeavour naturalists (today its scientific name is Artocarpus altilis). "This tree may be justly stiled the staff of life to these islanders," wrote Parkinson in his journal.

Artocarpus incisa, Left
=Sitodium altile.
otaheite

Sydney Parkinson pinxt 1769.

BREADFRUIT, TAHITI

NEW ZEALAND HONEYSUCKLE, NEW ZEALAND

TAHITIAN PLUM, TAHITI

Honeysuckle trees bearing fragrant
blossoms like those above grew more than
100 feet high at Tolaga Bay, where Cook
stopped in October 1769. The naturalists
labeled the tree Brabejum sparsum,
but it is now called Knightia excelsa.
The stately tree at right retains the
scientific name, Spondias dulcis, given it
by the expedition. "It is a very
wholesome and palatable fruit," Parkinson
said, "and makes excellent pies."

RED-RUMPED PARROT, TAHITI

These delicately colored sketches of South Seas birds are typical of more than 30 executed by Parkinson. After the completion of each sketch, the feathered skin was preserved in alcohol for the long return journey to England.

PURPLE-CROWNED PIGEON, TAHITI

Phaëton. erubescens.

RED-TAILED TROPIC BIRD, NEW ZEALAND COAST

138

Parkinson drew 156 fish caught by the Endeavour crewmen for Banks. Once a fish had been netted in the ship's seine—or harpooned with an iron-tipped spear—it was immediately brought to Parkinson, who sketched its outline in pencil, and added only a few washes of color. Later, working from notes made while the specimen was still fresh, he added details of the creature's fins and scales to complete the study.

GREEN MOON WRASSE, TAHITI

HONEYCOMB ROCK COD, TAHITI

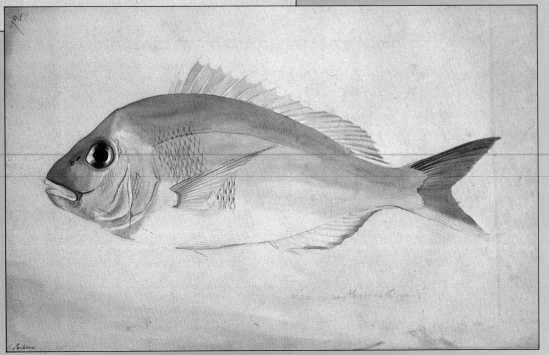

SNAPPER, NEW ZEALAND

CARPET SHARK, NEW ZEALAND

Chapter 5
Clearing up the final mysteries

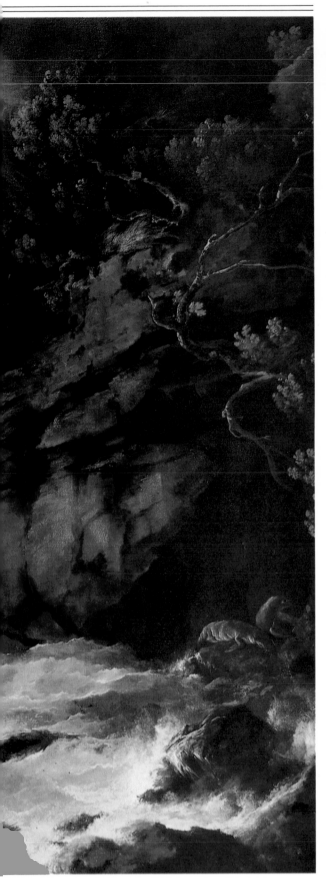

 had ambition not only to go farther than any one had been before," James Cook once wrote, "but as far as it was possible for man to go." To such a person, a homecoming could never be more than a pause in which to take new aim at the unknown. Indeed, even before the *Endeavour* had arrived back in England after three years of highly productive wandering, Cook was deep in schemes for a new voyage that he hoped would remove the remaining mysteries of the southern Pacific Ocean.

He had already proved that, aside from the great island of Australia, no continental land mass existed in the tropical and temperate zones of the South Pacific. Nevertheless, vast areas to the south and east of New Zealand remained uncharted. Shrouded in cold and fog and regularly beset by shrieking gales, these areas had defied navigators since Magellan's day. It was in here that Terra Australis Incognita might lie. Cook had strong doubts about the continent, but he maintained it would be "a great pitty that this thing which at times has been the object of many ages and Nations should not be wholy clear'd up."

As the *Endeavour* slogged toward home, Cook sketched his ideas in a report to the Admiralty: "I hope it will not be taken a miss if I give it as my opinion that the most feasible Method of making further discoveries in the South Sea is to enter it by the way of New Zealand." He proposed "first touching and refreshing at the Cape of Good Hope," then proceeding south of Australia to Queen Charlotte's Sound, New Zealand, "where again refresh Wood and Water." From there, he said, the expedition could run before the prevailing westerlies toward Cape Horn "in as high a Latitude as you please"—that is, as far south as desired—to search for land. Inventively, Cook suggested how the expedition could make two sweeps through the South Pacific during successive antarctic summers: If winter approached and no land had been sighted, Cook would "haul to the northward" and use islands already discovered as forward bases to rest and reprovision before resuming his search.

It was a masterful plan. What Cook had outlined was a circumnavigation of the globe from west to east in the colder latitudes—interrupting the voyage, if necessary, to swing up to Tahiti, where he knew he would be welcomed. From the tropics, he could double back to the west—using the prevailing easterlies in those warmer latitudes—in order to resume the huge counterclockwise circuit without leaving any gaps.

By early October, 1772, the Admiralty, anxious to strengthen England's claim to the discoveries of the *Endeavour*'s voyage, approved the idea essentially as Cook had outlined it, adding only a request that he

Angry seas and squall-spawned waterspouts off New Zealand threaten the Resolution, James Cook's command ship for his second voyage to the Pacific. Expedition artist William Hodges embellished this scene with a burning Maori fortress (background) and a fanciful local family, but the storm's violence was real enough, alarming the most experienced seamen aboard.

investigate reports of land sighted in the South Atlantic and the southern Indian Ocean. Cook immediately began preparations for a late-spring departure. Remembering the woes of the Great Barrier Reef, he asked for two ships this time, and the Navy assented. The *Endeavour* had been honorably retired from exploring, but at Cook's suggestion two similar craft were purchased, both colliers: the 462-ton *Resolution* and the 340-ton *Adventure*. Cook would command the *Resolution*, while the other ship would sail under Tobias Furneaux, a seasoned naval officer who had accompanied Wallis on his 1766 circumnavigation.

Once again the expedition would undertake a number of scientific experiments for the Royal Society. An astronomer was assigned to each ship—William Wales to the *Resolution* and William Bayly to her consort. Wales and Bayly would have charge of some new instruments designed to solve the navigator's age-old problem of reckoning longitude: seagoing chronometers. British clockmakers had long been trying to fulfill the Royal Society's demands for an accurate mariner's timepiece *(pages 146-147)*, and now four prototypes, resembling overgrown pocket watches, were to get their sea trials on Cook's voyage.

Cook was hoping that the *Endeavour*'s gentleman-adventurer, Joseph Banks, would join him again, and indeed Banks was counting on it. "O how Glorious would it be to set my heel upon the Pole and turn myself around 360 degrees in a second," Banks had written a friend. Fame had made the 29-year-old naturalist more extravagant than ever. For his second journey to the South Seas he wanted to bring Solander again, plus an entourage of 15 more, including a portrait painter, other artists, secretaries, servants and—to help while away the hours—two horn-playing musicians rigged out in scarlet-and-silver uniforms. Informed that the *Resolution* had no space for his small army of aides and attendants, Banks airily proposed that the ship be enlarged. When the Navy balked, he appealed to his good friend the Earl of Sandwich, First Lord of the Admiralty, and forthwith the *Resolution* was taken to the naval yard at Sheerness, where the alterations were made: An extra deck was added to the ship, together with a roundhouse on top.

Cook, though privately worried that the extra deck would make the *Resolution* top-heavy and therefore unseaworthy, went along with the changes out of friendship for Banks. Others were less agreeable. One of Cook's lieutenants, Charles Clerke, wrote to Banks, "By God, I'll go to sea in a grog-tub, if required, or in the *Resolution* as soon as you please, but must say I think her by far the most unsafe ship I ever saw or heard of." Then the pilot assigned to sail her to the Downs pronounced the *Resolution* unfit for any kind of sea duty and even refused to take her out of the shipyard, fearing she would capsize. That was enough. The Navy ordered the *Resolution* restored to her original state. When Banks next saw her, recalled a midshipman, "he swore and stamp'd upon the Wharf, like a Mad Man." Banks complained to Sandwich, making the mistake of lecturing the First Lord on naval construction. This time Sandwich did not budge, and Banks withdrew from the expedition, retinue and all.

In Banks's stead the Admiralty appointed John Reinhold Forster, a humorless Scottish-German naturalist, to catalogue the flora and fauna found along the way. William Hodges, a gifted landscape painter *(pages*

Tobias Furneaux, captain of the vessel that accompanied Cook on his second voyage, was a competent mariner with a well-deserved reputation for courage. But he lacked Cook's curiosity and, as a result, made a disappointing explorer.

6-13), was signed on as the expedition's official artist. The *Resolution's* crew included 16 veterans of the voyage of the *Endeavour*, all of whom had volunteered to sail with Cook a second time. Finally, Cook asked for and received a pair of seamen who had served on whalers that regularly cruised off Greenland, men experienced in navigating among ice floes.

Concerned as ever with his crew's health and the prevention of scurvy, Cook requisitioned special provisions from the Navy's Victualing Board. In addition to her normal stores of biscuit, salt beef and pork, spirits and suet, the *Resolution* was stocked with nearly 20,000 pounds of sauerkraut, 30 gallons of carrot marmalade, several jars of lemon and orange syrup for serious scurvy cases, and a hefty supply of Dr. James' Fever Powders, an 18th Century cure-all for minor aches and sicknesses.

Cook sailed from Plymouth on July 13, 1772, fourteen weeks later than he had intended, but satisfied with his ship and crew. On reaching Madeira—where he stopped to buy onions, wine and other fresh stores—he wrote the Admiralty that the *Resolution* "steers, works, sails well," and he also offered a wry postscript to the Banks affair. For more than three months, until just before the ships' arrival, a mysterious visitor in Madeira, named Burnett, had been waiting to join Banks as his botanical assistant. However, Cook noted with amusement, "Every part of Mr. Burnett's behavior and every action tended to prove that he was a Woman. I have not met with a person that entertains a doubt of a contrary nature." Apparently the raffish Banks was hoping to emulate his naturalist predecessor, Philibert Commerson, who had smuggled his lady friend, Jeanne Baret, aboard Bougainville's *Étoile*, in 1766. In the nick of time, Banks had notified his protégé not to join the expedition.

As the ships continued south, Cook instituted the same strict regimen of diet and cleanliness that had proved so beneficial for the men of the *Endeavour*. Furneaux in the *Adventure* was not so thoroughgoing, but both the *Resolution* and the *Adventure* arrived in Capetown with healthy crews. In the Dutch port, Forster, who had brought his son, George, along as an assistant, persuaded Cook to take on yet another naturalist, an energetic Swedish doctor named Anders Sparrman.

With the coming of the Southern Hemisphere's spring in November 1772, the *Resolution* and the *Adventure* weighed anchor and headed for antarctic waters. Their destination was Cape Circumcision, the headland in the South Atlantic sighted in 1739 by the French mariner Lozier Bouvet, who claimed it was the tip of a Southern continent. About 100 miles south of Capetown, in lat. 35° S., the weather became bitter cold and Cook issued fearnought jackets and trousers and red baize caps. For a week a hard westerly gale raged, prompting young Forster to bemoan the *Resolution's* "prodigious rolling," which "daily made great havoc among cups, saucers, glasses, bottles, dishes, plates, and everything that was moveable." The gale was the expedition's first sample of polar sailing—a mild foretaste of what Cook's men would experience later.

At lat. 51° S. the ships plunged into the subantarctic world of drifting ice and driving sleet. On December 11 the *Resolution* approached an iceberg so large that the sailors initially mistook it for a looming cliff. A midshipman later commented on the deceptiveness of icebergs: "When

In Tahiti, the able but irascible naturalist John Forster holds a bird while it is sketched by his precocious son, George. Not yet 18 when he embarked on Cook's voyage, George was already a gifted artist, scientist and teacher.

the Sun shines and the sky is clear they are of a fine light blue and transparent. In bad dirty weather they resemble Land covered with snow, the lower part appearing black.''

The ships were now southeast of Bouvet's reported position for Cape Circumcision. Cook was awed by the polar seas. On calm days, he noted, penguins cavorted at the edges of the floating ice mountains. But when the wind increased, the swells rapidly built up and dwarfed the 60-foot-high bergs, breaking "quite over them, such was the force and height of the waves, which for a few moments is pleasing to the eye, but when one reflects on the danger this occasions, the mind is fill'd with horror, for was a ship to get against the weather side of one of these islands when the sea runs high she would be dashed to pieces in a moment.''

On December 14 the *Resolution* ran up against a barrier of pack ice. Cook supposed that "there is land behind it,'' and therefore cruised parallel to its edge, seeking a way through to the shore. Fog closed in so thickly at one point that it was impossible to see the bowsprit from the afterdeck. When the mists cleared, Cook found that whales were frolicking beneath the *Resolution's* bow and "our Rigging and sail were all decorated with icikles.'' After skirting the pack for 90 miles he turned north. Still there was no sign of Bouvet's cape, only the Gargantuan "floating rocks,'' some of which were more than two miles in circumference.

Approaching antarctic waters in January 1773, crewmen on Cook's vessels haul aboard chunks of icebergs, which would be melted for drinking water. A gunner's mate said the work made "arms put on the appearance of icicles," but Cook, whose ships took on nearly 25 tons of the ice in less than six hours, pronounced it "the most expeditious way of watering I ever met with."

On Christmas Day, Cook resumed a tradition he had established on his first voyage. After bringing the *Resolution* "under a very snug sail lest I should be surprised with a gale of wind and a drunken crew," he issued extra rations of rum to the sailors. That evening, after a rousing dinner, the *Adventure* "rainged alongside of us and gave us three Cheers." Throughout the following week the two ships remained close together, probing fields of loose ice and searching for Cape Circumcision. All the while, the naturalists were observing a variety of antarctic birds, including petrels, albatrosses and scores of penguins. One day the crews of both ships lined the rails to be entertained by the military behavior of a group of penguins on an ice floe. "They seemed to perform their Evolutions so well," recalled an officer, "that they only wanted the use of Arms to cut a figure on Whimbleton Common." Penguins were thought to be evidence of nearby land; but the horizon was empty, and a 150-fathom lead line failed to touch bottom.

On January 3, 1773, Cook gave up looking for Cape Circumcision, stating his opinion that Bouvet had seen "nothing but Mountains of ice surrounded by field Ice." (Bouvet had in fact discovered a tiny, remote isle that later was named for him: Cook had simply missed it—understandably, since Bouvet Island is only 22 square miles in area.)

No sooner did Cook bear east—to search for a body of land sighted by the French explorer Yves de Kerguelen in 1772—than he made an important discovery about the behavior of the pack ice: It was steadily drifting to the east, and therefore it could not be attached to any land mass. Pondering how icebergs originated and how polar ice fields were formed, Cook wanted to know "what effect cold has on sea water in some of the following instances: does it freeze or does it not, if it does, what degree of cold is necessary and what becomes of the salt brine? for all the ice we meet with yields water perfectly sweet and fresh." John Forster correctly predicted that salt water freezes into nonsalty ice under certain conditions, and asserted that the presence of an ice pack does not necessarily imply the existence of a polar land mass. Cook eventually agreed.

After an unsuccessful week searching for Kerguelen's island, Cook resumed his southerly course, and on January 17 the men on the *Resolution* and the *Adventure* became the first ever to cross the Antarctic Circle. That evening, at lat. 67° 15′ S., the lookout at the masthead gazed out upon a formidable panorama of icebergs, 38 in all. "Soon after," wrote Cook, "we discovered Feild or Packed Ice in the same Direction and had so many loose pieces about the ship that we were obliged to loof for one and bear up for another." He concluded that it was not "consistant with the safty of the Sloops or any ways prudent for me to perservere in going farther," and changed course to the northeast, reluctantly giving up the southward probe. It is now known that the *Resolution* was at that moment only 75 miles from the coast of Antarctica.

In a thick fog on February 8, Furneaux and the *Adventure* disappeared. Cook spent two days searching for the ship, firing a signal gun every 30 minutes—but there was no sign of her. He was not concerned, for he and Furneaux had agreed to rendezvous at New Zealand's Queen Charlotte's Sound. Assuming that Furneaux would go there directly, Cook headed east, along the 60th parallel, in uncharted waters.

The ship was still hedged all around by a thicket of "ice islands," as Cook called the largest bergs. He marveled at the "curious and romantick views many of these islands exhibit." Once a berg three or four hundred feet high turned bottom up near the *Resolution*; another one, four times as big as the ship, shattered silently into pieces as they passed. Boulder-sized chunks of floating ice, which the men called "plumpers" because of the way they bumped against the ship's hull, could be even more dangerous than the ice islands, wrote Cook. "The latter," he explained, "are generally seen at a sufficient distance to give time to steer clear of them, whereas the others cannot be seen till they are under the Bows."

On March 17, Cook headed northeast and made for New Zealand. He had been in polar latitudes for four months and among icebergs for more than three. Ten days later the *Resolution* reached the southwest corner of New Zealand's South Island and put into a capacious inlet he called Dusky Sound. He had sailed 11,000 miles since leaving Capetown.

Mooring his ship to shore-front trees in a deep and sheltered cove of Dusky Sound, Cook set about refreshing the crew and making repairs. He remained at anchor for more than five weeks. The naturalists studied birds in the magnificently forested wilderness and tried to communicate with the local inhabitants, who were too shy to board the ship. Cook brewed spruce beer from the needles of a native tree and sent out hunting parties for other foods to help cure the *Resolution's* few incipient scurvy cases. On May 11 he was at sea again and a week later reached Queen Charlotte's Sound. There, as expected, he found the *Adventure*.

Furneaux had been waiting at Queen Charlotte's Sound for more than a month. With the Southern Hemisphere's winter at hand, he had snugged down the *Adventure* for a long stay, and had set up a small encampment ashore for his sick crewmen, several of whom had severe cases of scurvy and were not improving. But a winter respite in New Zealand was not included in Cook's rigorous timetable. After placing the scurvy-weakened *Adventure* seamen on a strict diet of wild celery and other fresh food, he informed Furneaux that the ships would sail in a week or two. Their course would be due east, between lat. 41° and 46° S. for 2,000 miles; then, at long. 140° W., they would head north to Tahiti to refresh. This route would take the *Resolution* and the *Adventure* 100 to 350 miles south of the track Cook had followed from Tahiti to New Zealand on the *Endeavour* in 1769.

"It may be thought by some an extraordinary step in me to proceed on discoveries as far south as 46° in the very depth of Winter," Cook commented in his journal, "for it must be own'd that this is a Season by no means favorable for discoveries." But, because his plans called for him to explore even farther to the south when the Southern Hemisphere's spring rolled around in October, he considered it essential to complete this leg of the voyage now; otherwise, a belt of the Southern ocean wide enough to hide Terra Australis would go unexamined.

They sailed on June 7—and soon were plunging through haze, rain and a succession of gales. Twice the *Resolution's* wheel bucked so violently in the heavy seas that it flung the steersmen across the deck. However, the easterly leg of the passage was completed without serious harm to men or ships. It also yielded no signs of land, thus eliminating

Mr. Kendall's wonderful watch

Perhaps the most highly prized item of equipment taken on Cook's second voyage in 1772 was a novel timepiece that the captain fondly called "Mr. Kendall's Watch Machine." That instrument—the first dependable chronometer carried into the Pacific—enabled Cook to determine longitude far more quickly than had ever been possible before.

Larcum Kendall, the watchmaker to whom Cook was referring, was actually the beneficiary of a long line of scientists and inventors. The principle for figuring out longitude had been postulated as early as 1474. That year a German astronomer named Regiomontanus noted that, because the earth rotates 360 degrees in 24 hours, or 15 degrees per hour, a mariner who knew both local time and the time at his point of departure could calculate the number of degrees he had traveled west of his starting point by multiplying the difference between the times by 15.

Navigators could readily ascertain local time by using optical devices to measure the angle of the sun or stars above the horizon. But keeping track of the time at the point of departure was quite another matter. A clock was the most obvious means for doing so, but on an extended voyage any known clock would be rendered inaccurate by changes in temperature that caused expansion or contraction of its metal works.

By the beginning of the 18th Century, the British Parliament had come to regard precise, long-range navigation as a matter of such importance that it offered the splendid sum of £20,000—an amount that would support a Briton in style for life—to anyone who solved the longitude problem. The reward, to be awarded by a body of specialists designated the Board of Longitude, went begging for nearly half a century—but not for lack of interest; indeed, the painter Hogarth, satirizing the national preoccupation with the subject in 1736, portrayed a lunatic working away at the longitude problem in a madhouse.

In 1752 Tobias Mayer, a German astronomer, devised a set of lunar tables for computing longitude at sea by means of optical observations alone. A French navigator used these tables aboard Louis Antoine de Bougainville's *Boudeuse* in 1766 (page 90), and Cook himself calculated longitude by this system on his first Pacific voyage. But the method was so immensely complicated that even a skilled mathematician required four hours to get a reading. Few sea captains had either the specialized knowledge or the inclination to bother with the lunar method, and eventually

Britain's Board of Longitude rejected it as a candidate for the reward.

The genius who came up with a truly practical way to compute east-west travel was a self-educated carpenter-turned-clockmaker named John Harrison, who took the problem on as his life's work in 1714, when he was 21 years old. When he finally found the solution after 45 years, it was brilliantly simple: a clock with a balance wheel made of an amalgam of steel and brass. Because those metals expand with heat and contract with cold at different rates that compensate for each other, they kept the clock ticking at a steady pace whatever the temperature.

In 1759 Harrison eagerly laid his invention before the Board of Longitude, which successfully tested it on a voyage to Barbados in 1764. Alas for Harrison, Parliament was not so openhanded now, and he waited 14 years to collect all of his £20,000 reward.

He won it in the end, but the Board of Longitude had meanwhile commissioned Larcum Kendall to duplicate Harrison's watch. The copy, encased in silver and daintily enameled, was ready when Cook embarked on his second voyage in 1772. Thus Kendall, not Harrison, won credit in the logs of Captain Cook.

Cook used this four-inch watch to fix Pacific longitudes.

the last temperate-zone area of the South Pacific from the list of possible locations of Terra Australis. The run to the north was peaceful—until the morning of August 16, when the vessels were just off Tahiti.

The first light of dawn that day revealed the *Resolution* to be dangerously close to a reef in a dead calm, and the sea was carrying her toward it. Moreover, the water was too deep for anchoring. Arriving on deck, Cook began shouting commands immediately, and boats were put out to try towing the *Resolution* seaward, but the ship continued drifting— and a short distance off her starboard bow the *Adventure* was in similar trouble. To make matters worse, Tahitians, male and female, had paddled their canoes out to the vessels and were clambering aboard to greet the Englishmen. Stamping back and forth, Cook shouted to the islanders to get out of the way and ordered his men to keep the decks clear.

Windless, stifling hours passed as the ships inched closer to destruction, carried by incoming seas too strong for the sweating oarsmen to overcome. Again and again the lead line was heaved and failed to reach bottom. Then the *Resolution's* stern struck a coral head with a terrible jarring crunch, and struck it again with each fall of the ocean swell. The ship crashed against the reef with such violence, wrote astronomer Wales, that "it was with difficulty some times that we kept on our legs." At this moment, with shipwreck imminent, one of the anchors caught bottom and provided a purchase that enabled the crew to pull the vessel back into deep water. But now a new peril arose: The *Adventure* was drifting down on the motionless *Resolution*. Only 10 yards separated the converging ships when the *Adventure* finally managed to stay herself with an anchor. In midafternoon a slight wind carried both vessels comfortably offshore; they later sailed to a safe anchorage.

Emotionally drained by the event, Cook went to his cabin, accompanied by the Swedish naturalist Sparrman, who later recalled that the captain was in much pain. "Although he had from beginning to end of the incident appeared perfectly alert and able, he was suffering so greatly from his stomach that he was in a great sweat and could scarcely stand. It was, indeed, hardly remarkable that, after so great a responsibility and so prodigious a strain on both his mental and physical capacities, he should be completely exhausted." Sparrman persuaded Cook to take a dose of brandy, and the commander seemed to relax. Over the years his unshakable coolness at times of crisis had amazed his officers and men. But now the strain of Cook's work was beginning to take its toll.

The expedition spent only two weeks in Tahiti, long enough to repair the *Resolution* and cure the scurvy cases. On September 1 the ships sailed for the neighboring Society Islands, 100 miles to the east of Tahiti, where the *Endeavour* had been warmly received four years earlier. Cook called first at Huahine and then at Raiatea. In both places he was greeted hospitably, receiving abundant gifts of hogs and fruit; "our decks were so full of them," wrote Cook, "that we could hardly move." When the ships departed on September 17, they took with them two Society Islanders: On the *Adventure* was a man named Mae (pronounced "my") who henceforth was known as Omai; the *Resolution* carried a youth named Hitihiti—modified to Odiddy by the crew.

Although Cook had intended to head south to New Zealand along the route he had taken in the *Endeavour,* he now decided to "direct my course to the west, inclining to the south to avoid the tracks of former navigators." Eventually, he predicted, he would get into the latitude of the islands that Tasman had called Amsterdam and Middleburg—the Tongas. On the way he passed some uninhabited atolls that he named after a friend, Captain Hervey; one of them is still called Hervey Island today, being part of what is known as the Cook Islands.

Reaching the Tongas on October 1, Cook learned that the local name for Middleburg was Eua, and for Amsterdam, Tongatabu. He also found that the inhabitants were exceptionally open and generous, and he dubbed the whole archipelago that included the Tongas the Friendly Islands. The islanders' good-natured filching had not changed since Tasman's day, however. Astronomer Wales waded ashore carrying his shoes and lost them moments later to a thief who escaped barefoot over sharp coral rocks. Another Tongan lifted some navigational books from the *Resolution* and sped off in a canoe; when one of the ship's boats gave chase, he dived into the water and swam triumphantly away.

Ashore, Cook sampled an alcoholic drink called kava, and also discovered that the Tongans had an enormous predilection for iron nails. They eagerly traded great amounts of food and a commodity the Europeans had not seen before, red feathers from the red-breasted musk parrot, for "not less than three or four hundred weight from the largest spike down to a six-penny nail." He remarked on the Tongans' custom of touching everything they received to their heads "by way of thanks," and took note of their peculiar practice of cutting off parts of their little fingers, presumably in propitiation of the gods.

With spring at hand, Cook set sail for New Zealand, where he would prepare to resume his exploration. Land was sighted on October 21, but before the *Resolution* could enter Cook Strait a gale struck with such fury that the ship was obliged to beat against the storm for 13 days; it did not reach the shelter of Queen Charlotte's Sound until November 3.

During the gale the *Adventure* had disappeared again. By the time Cook was ready to begin his second sweep through the high latitudes of the South Pacific three weeks later, there still was no sign of her. Cook was concerned, but not alarmed. "I can only suppose," he wrote, "that Captain Furneaux being tired of beating against the northwest winds had taken resolution to make the best of his way to Cape Horn" and back to England. On the chance that the *Adventure* might yet make it to Queen Charlotte's Sound, Cook left a note in a bottle buried under a marked tree; it outlined the *Resolution's* general route but cautioned, "as Captain Cook has not the least hope of meeting with Captain Furneaux he will take not upon him to name any place for a Rendezvous."

On November 26 the *Resolution* set off to the southeast alone. Cook's subsequent traversal of the southern Pacific, in a series of zigzagging probes, was his second great antarctic excursion. While it did not last as long as the first, it penetrated much farther toward the Pole. By December 12 he was engulfed in fields of loose ice. Three days later, while picking a path through the bergs at lat. 66° S., just outside the Antarctic Circle, the *Resolution* drifted down on a great ice island whose crest loomed to twice the height of her mastheads. Her stern barely missed the

Omai, a Society Islander carried to England by the Adventure, clutches a stool and other Polynesian articles in his tattooed hands. After his arrival in London in 1774, he attended balls, met the illustrious and even inspired a successful theater production. He returned to the Society Islands three years later in Western dress, creating an equal sensation among his countrymen.

A press-fanned furor that led to ruin

Perhaps the most gifted pupil of Captain Cook was George Vancouver, who shipped out with the great explorer as a 15-year-old midshipman in 1772 and thereafter devoted his life to the Royal Navy. In the 1790s he crowned his career with his own four-year Pacific voyage of exploration, during which he circumnavigated the large Canadian island now named for him; until then, it was thought to be a peninsula.

At the time, Vancouver's achievement was overshadowed by an imbroglio over a truculent young midshipman named Thomas Pitt, whom he sent home in midvoyage for an unrecorded transgression. Pitt was a cousin of the Prime Minister, William Pitt. Soon after Vancouver returned to England in 1795 young Pitt alleged that

Vancouver had flogged him (the Navy barred the flogging of midshipmen), and challenged the explorer to a duel.

Declining to fight, Vancouver proposed an official review of the charges, which he neither denied nor admitted. The Admiralty investigated but did not reveal its findings. Meanwhile, the newspapers feasted on the dispute, generally favoring the wellborn Pitt. The furor effectively put an end to Vancouver's career; he retired to obscurity and two years later died at the age of 40. Had he lived longer, Vancouver might have had vindication; many other officers also found Pitt insubordinate, and he was eventually booted out of the Navy in spite of his family connection.

Vancouver missed an even deeper

satisfaction. After his death Britain and the United States argued for decades over sovereignty of the Pacific coast between Oregon and Alaska. In 1846 an international commission finally decided in Britain's favor, placing the border at the 49th parallel, with a loop around the bottom of Vancouver Island. The decision was based on Vancouver's precise charts, which substantiated Britain's claim and thus won a Pacific coastline for her North American dominions.

Thomas Pitt swings a cane at Captain George Vancouver in a savage cartoon that made Vancouver appear to be at fault.

ice. It was "the most Miraculous escape from being every soul lost that ever man had," wrote one midshipman. And Cook, who had withstood too many such scares, dryly wrote in his journal: "According to the old proverb a miss is as good as a mile, but our situation requires more misses than we can expect." Accordingly, he hauled off to the north.

Five days later the ice cleared and Cook turned south again, crossing the Antarctic Circle on December 20. With the weather worsening, the men were reissued their fearnought jackets. The cold became so intense, wrote Cook, that "Our ropes were like wires, Sails like board or plates of Metal and the sheaves froze fast in the blocks so that it required our utmost effort to get a Top-sail down and up."

But morale was high. On Christmas Day, their second at sea, the *Resolution*'s men broke out several months' rations of brandy that they had saved for the occasion and, wrote Sparrman, joked "that if they were wrecked on any of the 168 masses of ice surrounding us they would certainly die happy and content." That day Cook turned north to cover an unexplored swath of ocean southeast of Tahiti. After finding no land he headed east for nearly 1,000 miles, then south again, to the consternation of those in the crew who had thought Cook would maintain his eastward course around Cape Horn and home.

Undeterred by the prospects of rough weather, or by his own fatigue, Cook pressed southward. "Excessive hard gales" now assaulted the *Resolution*, and on January 15, 1774, a tremendous wave struck the ship abeam, sweeping across the deck, crashing through the skylights and flooding the cabin with icy water. Cook ordered the water pumped out, and kept going. For days blizzards whipped the sea; the amazed Odiddy called the snow "white rain." Then the temperature rose slightly, causing a thick fog that forced the *Resolution* to lay to.

On January 30, at lat. 71° 10′, Cook could go no farther. Facing the *Resolution* was an impenetrable ice field in which "we counted Ninety Seven Ice Hills or Mountains, many of them vastly large. I will not say it was impossible anywhere to get in among the Ice, but I will assert that the bare attempting of it would be a very dangerous enterprise and what I believe no man in my situation would have thought of." Ruefully, he gave the order to come about. At that moment one of the *Resolution*'s midshipmen, George Vancouver, who would one day become a renowned explorer on his own, clambered out to the tip of the bowsprit and, waving his hat, shouted "*Ne plus ultra!*" ("None farther!"). For the rest of his life Vancouver liked to boast that he had been nearer the South Pole than any other man.

As he recrossed the Antarctic Circle and bore northeast, Cook knew that he had eradicated the last possibility of a habitable continent in the South Pacific. The myth of Terra Australis Incognita was at an end. Beyond where he had sailed there might be land, but it could not be the paradise of de Brosses and Dalrymple, covered with lush forests and fertile river valleys and peopled by millions. If land existed, it would be desolate and icebound, covered with endless snow and populated by penguins. (Such a land did, of course, exist—but no man set foot on Antarctica for almost half a century more.)

His instructions totally fulfilled, Cook could now have turned toward home. He did not. Characteristically, he wrote that "although I had proved there was no Continent there remained room for very large Islands, in places wholly unexplored and many of those formerly discovered are but imperfectly explored. For me at this time to have quited this Ocean, with a good Ship, expressly sent out on discoveries, a healthy crew and not in want of either Stores or Provisions, would have been betraying not only a want of perseverance, but judgement, in supposeing the South Pacific Ocean to have been so well explored that nothing remained to be done in it." He resolved to make a second counterclockwise sweep through the tropics, beginning with a search for a group of islands sighted far to the southeast of Tahiti by Spanish mariner Juan Fernández in the 16th Century. Then Cook hoped to touch at Easter Island, first sighted by the Dutch explorer Roggeveen in 1722, before sailing to Tahiti. Finally Cook would visit Quirós' Austrialia del Espíritu Santo, 1,160 miles to the west of the Tongas, which the explorer Bougainville claimed to have seen in 1768.

Setting a course to the north, Cook aimed for the area indicated by Juan Fernández, but did not find the islands named for the Spaniard. On February 25, Cook gave up the search. At this point his rugged constitution broke down, and he succumbed to what he described as "the Billious colick and so Violent as to confine me to my bed." He had been pale and lean for more than two months, but his collapse took the crew of the *Resolution* by surprise. For a week he hovered at the brink of death, vomiting, hiccuping, barely responding to the surgeon's hot baths and stomach plasters. The ship's company was plunged into gloom. A hot soup made from the fresh meat of a ship's dog finally helped bring him around. There were smiles and sighs of relief throughout the vessel.

His health improving, Cook anchored off Easter Island on March 12. Like previous explorers, the English gaped at the colossal stone statues that brood over the island's slopes. However, little food and water were available, and after only four days the *Resolution* set sail, arriving on April 6 in the Marquesas, the lovely eastern Pacific archipelago discovered by Alvaro de Mendaña in 1595 and not seen since. Cook traded for provisions with the slim, lithe and light-skinned inhabitants until one of the sailors offered them red feathers from the batch picked up in Tonga. All trade instantly ceased, because the Marquesans, who regarded the feathers as sacred, would accept no other payment and Cook had too few feathers to go around. Hastening on to the southwest now, he passed through the northern Tuamotu Islands, and a few days later discovered a small group of atolls that he called the Palliser Islands for Hugh Palliser, an old friend and benefactor who was now Comptroller of the Navy. On April 22 he anchored once again in Matavai Bay in Tahiti.

Although Cook planned to stay only a few days in Tahiti, the exuberance with which the islanders welcomed him and the abundance of fresh food—some of it purchased with Tongan red feathers, which the Society Islanders also prized—persuaded him to linger three weeks. The high point was the sight of a mighty fleet of fully manned war canoes, more than 300 of them, which the Tahitians had assembled to attack a neighboring island. Many of the canoes were double-hulled, adorned with flags and streamers and fitted out with broad decks aft for warriors and their arsenals of spears, clubs and piles of stones. Cook was also shown a shipyard where the Tahitians were building a double-hulled war canoe 108 feet in length, as long as the *Resolution*. Leaving Tahiti, he called at the nearby islands of Huahine and Raiatea—where he deposited a tearful Odiddy and took on more provisions.

On June 4, Cook left the Society Islands to continue the westward leg of his second sweep through the tropics. En route, he recognized an atoll that Wallis had called Lord Howe's Island—now known as Mopihaa—and came upon an uncharted speck of land that he named for Lord Palmerston of the Admiralty. A third island, sighted on June 20, seemed likely to offer refreshment, but when Cook went ashore his party was attacked by a crowd of Polynesians who hurled rocks and spears, one missile just missing Cook's shoulder. Retreating hurriedly, he named it Savage Island; today it is called Niue.

Moving on to the west, the *Resolution* stopped again in the Tongas, this time for three days. Again the English got a warm welcome. At one point even Cook—a highly moral man who had so far adhered to his marriage vows—was almost unable to resist the advances of a Polynesian beauty who was offered to him on the beach by an older woman. But his honor held firm, and he tried to extricate himself by saying he had no nails to give the young woman and was loath to part with the shirt on his back. The older female then vilified him, "sneering in my face and saying, what sort of a man are you thus to refuse the embraces of so fine a young woman, for the girl certainly did not want beauty which I could however withstand, but the abuse of the old Woman I could not and therefore hastned into the Boat."

He now steered northwest for Quirós' islands. Running under full sail during the day but with only topsails at night lest he miss his landfall, he followed a track just a few miles south of the one taken by Bougainville in 1768. On July 16 he came to Bougainville's Aurora island, the north-easternmost member of the 400-mile-long archipelago that included Espíritu Santo and had been named the Great Cyclades by the French. Cook renamed the chain the New Hebrides and remained there for six weeks, charting the islands.

Bypassing Aurora but determined to explore the whole archipelago, Cook sailed south until his men sighted a harbor on a heavily wooded island named Malekula. Men came out in canoes, and a few of them ventured on board. Others, however, shot arrows at the ship and had to be turned back with musket fire over their heads. Cook decided to land anyway and used a procedure that he had come to rely on to ensure against misunderstandings: Approaching the beach in one of the ship's boats, he leaped into the water alone and, holding a green branch in his hand to signify friendship, strode ashore. The fearless greeting worked; he was welcomed in a friendly fashion and given permission to cut firewood. But the islanders were not interested in the presents Cook offered and would not trade for food or allow the English to come much inland from the beach. Like the people who had been so intractable toward Quirós and later to Bougainville, they were Melanesians—short, dark-skinned and curly-haired, and of a less inquisitive temperament than the Polynesians.

In a Tahitian fleet of war canoes and sail-equipped transports encountered by Cook, the ranking chief (left) is wearing an enormous wicker headdress haloed with feathers, and a feathered breast gorget. Many of the vessels bear carvings and totems that the Tahitian fighters have consecrated to Oro, god of war.

For the next 10 days Cook slowly cruised among the southern islands of the archipelago without going ashore. On August 4, in need of wood and fresh water, he decided to chance landing at an island called Erromanga. Again he stepped ashore carrying a green branch. A "great Multitude" looked at him with suspicion as he approached. A chief gave him a small amount of food and water in exchange for trinkets, then indicated he wanted Cook to haul his boat to the beach. Alarmed, Cook stepped back into the boat. The islanders surrounded it and tried to drag it ashore, while some of them began firing arrows and throwing stones. Cook tried shooting his musket over their heads, but it would not fire, and so he ordered his men to shoot. Four Erromangans were killed.

Back on the *Resolution* he mulled over the incident and decided he could understand why the islanders were hostile. "It is impossible for them to know our real design," he wrote. "We enter their Ports and attempt to land in a peaceable manner. If it succeeds all is well, if not we land nevertheless and maintain our footing by the Superiority of our firearms. In what other light can they first look upon us but as invaders of their Country?"

At the island of Tanna near the southern end of the New Hebrides chain, the expedition's reception was initially similar, but after a few guns had been fired into the air the inhabitants were cowed, and Cook was able to trade for food and obtain wood and water unmolested. From Tanna, he retraced his course back up the chain of islands, continuing his survey. On August 25 the *Resolution* finally came upon the largest island, which Cook recognized as Quirós' Espíritu Santo. Several days were spent examining the great Bay of St. Philip and St. James, the scene of Quirós' exultation and suffering. Gazing upon the island's high peaks, Cook could see how Quirós might think it was attached to "the Southern Continent which at that time and until very lately was supposed to exist." In respect for "that great Navigator," Cook named a nearby headland Cape Quirós before departing from the New Hebrides.

On a southerly course for New Zealand, he was surprised a few days later to encounter a large, previously undiscovered island. It was girded almost completely by reefs, but Cook found a way through and landed. He was met by cheerful and hospitable inhabitants who, though poor, did not steal. Moreover, the women would have nothing to do with the English sailors. Cook, who had never encountered this combination of honesty and chastity in the South Pacific, was enchanted by the people and spent three weeks mapping the east coast of the 300-mile-long island, which he called New Caledonia. He had discovered the South Pacific's fourth-largest island, one not seen before by any European explorer. By October 3 the *Resolution* was heading south again for New Zealand. Halfway there, Cook sighted another unknown isle—this one little more than a surf-beaten rock. He surveyed it and named it Norfolk Island. On October 18, 1774, the expedition was back in Queen Charlotte's Sound, having swept from the South Seas the last remaining will-o'-the-wisps of a great continental land mass.

Cook hastened to the spot where he had buried the bottle for Furneaux almost a year before. It was gone, and nothing had been left in its place. From the Maoris the English got confusing reports of killings. Only

His Majesty's sloop of war Resolution, here becalmed, served as Captain Cook's command ship on his second and third voyages. The 462-ton former collier, wrote Cook, "was the fittest for the service she was going upon of any I had ever seen."

Cook's epic sweeps to the ends of the ocean

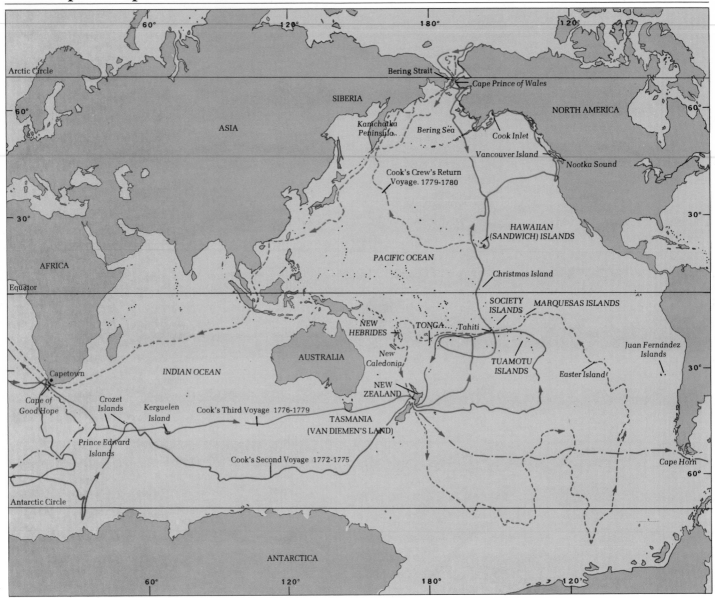

much later did Cook ascertain the fate of the *Adventure*. Driven far offshore by storms, Furneaux anchored in Queen Charlotte's Sound on November 30, 1773, just five days after Cook had left. Upon finding Cook's message, Furneaux spent some three weeks refitting for a voyage back to England. The day before his departure he sent out a boat with 10 men to gather vegetables. Their work done, the men began eating dinner on a beach. Some Maoris snatched their food, and the English opened fire, killing two. Incensed, the Maoris turned on the English and massacred all 10, then ate their remains. Furneaux judged the blame was shared by both sides and made no reprisals; instead he sailed for home, arriving in England in July 1774.

Cook's men thoroughly overhauled the *Resolution* in Queen Charlotte's Sound and weighed anchor on November 10. Cook had merely to

During his second voyage, Cook crisscrossed the South Seas from a base at New Zealand before heading home, east past Cape Horn and north along the coast of Africa. Returning in 1776, he probed from the same location for the elusive Northwest Passage across the top of North America. After Cook's death in 1779, the expedition searched again for the passage, then sailed south for the Cape of Good Hope and home.

set a course for Cape Horn and home. As was his wont, however, he added something else: sailing east across the South Pacific to the western end of the Strait of Magellan, then 360 miles down the bleak inlet-nicked coast to Cape Horn, mapping the shoreline extensively despite constant danger of being driven against it by the prevailing westerly winds. His third Christmas found him in a tiny inlet northwest of the tip of Tierra del Fuego. He rounded the Horn on December 29, entered the Strait of Le Maire, through which the *Endeavour* had passed in 1768, and charted the north coast of Staten Island.

As a coda to the voyage, he spent eight additional weeks examining the high-latitude waters of the South Atlantic, including one last spot where the imaginative geographer Dalrymple had envisioned a continental shore: Nothing was there. He reached the Cape of Good Hope on March 21 and, after a five-week rest, sailed for England, arriving on July 30, 1775. He had been away for three years and 18 days, had sailed more than 70,000 miles, and in his crisscrossing sweeps through the Southern latitudes he had discovered some 30 new islands, ranging in size from isolated specks of coral to the giant New Caledonia. He had rediscovered the long-lost Marquesas and Easter Island, charted the New Hebrides and erased Dalrymple's continent from the inhabitable zones of the Pacific. The expedition had also proved that a chronometer could be used to provide accurate navigational fixes; the *Resolution's* naturalist had brought back observations on an amazing variety of antarctic birds and fish; and once again, Cook had astounded the Admiralty by not losing a single man to scurvy.

There was no doubting, this time, who deserved the credit and the honor for the extraordinary voyage. Cook was promoted to captain and was made a Fellow of the Royal Society, which awarded him its Copley Medal for his work in combating scurvy. A recognized celebrity, he dined with the famous—including the voluble diarist James Boswell, who reported to his literary friend Dr. Samuel Johnson that, "while I was with the captain, I caught the enthusiasm of curiosity and adventure, and felt a strong inclination to go with him on his next voyage."

Cook was not sure he would be asked to make another voyage, and was of two minds about whether to accept if he were. The Navy had appointed him to an honorary post at Greenwich Hospital that brought a handsome pension. To his old employer John Walker he wrote that, although the *Resolution* was being readied for more exploration, "I shall not command her, my fate drives me from one extream to a nother. A few Months ago the whole Southern hemisphere was hardly big enough for me and now I am going to be confined within the limits of Greenwich Hospital, which are far too small for an active mind like mine."

His ship, in fact, was being refitted for a trip to the North Pacific. For generations, Britons had dreamed of the so-called Northwest Passage, a strait linking the Atlantic and the Pacific Oceans north of Canada. After years of searching, no outlet had been found on the Atlantic, but perhaps one could be traced from the Pacific. In early January, 1776, the Royal Society and the Navy agreed to equip a full-fledged examination of America's Pacific coast in quest of the strait. Who should lead the expedition? Cook certainly knew of the proposed voyage and had acted as a planning consultant, but he had not been offered the post of commander.

Because Cook would have to give up his pension if he sailed again, the Navy was reluctant to ask him directly. Instead, in February 1776 the First Lord of the Admiralty, Lord Sandwich, invited Cook to a dinner along with several other Naval leaders, including Comptroller Lord Palliser and Admiralty Secretary Philip Stephens. Sandwich outlined the new expedition and asked Cook whom he might suggest as commander. It was an artfully staged question. Cook's sense of duty and his irrepressible curiosity were aroused: He volunteered. "If I am not so fortunate as to make my passage home by the North Pole," he wrote to a friend, "I hope at least to determine whether it is practicable or not."

It was a disastrous mistake. At the age of 47, Cook was in good physical health, having recovered from his stomach illness. But without realizing it, he was psychologically exhausted. For seven years, while commanding two consecutive voyages of exploration, he had been under continual strain; he needed more than a mere six months or so of rest. From the outset of this voyage he would strike his veteran officers as a perceptibly different man. Along with his usual zeal, there were increasing signs of weariness and impatience and more frequent flashes of his fierce but hitherto controlled temper.

The *Resolution* also, alas, was not the superb vessel for exploration she had been. Hastily and incompetently refitted by the Navy—Cook was too busy with other matters to oversee the work properly—she would need frequent repairs.

In all other respects the expedition was well endowed. Once again the *Resolution* would be accompanied by a second collier, this one the *Discovery*, skippered by Charles Clerke, a capable veteran of both of Cook's previous voyages. The other officers were almost without exception of high caliber; they included a future admiral and a dozen captains-to-be—among them William Bligh, later accorded notoriety after a mutiny on a ship under his command, the *Bounty* (pages 162-163).

Cook sailed from Plymouth on July 12, 1776; Clerke and the *Discovery* followed a few weeks later and joined the expedition in Capetown. There, the *Resolution*, which had already proved to be leaky, was patched up. "If I return in the *Resolution*," wrote one officer in a letter home, "the next Trip I may Safely Venture in a Ship Built of Ginger Bread." By November 30 both ships were reprovisioned, and the expedition's livestock, which already included pigs, sheep, goats, rabbits and chickens, plus a few cows, a bull and even a peacock, was augmented by four horses. The Polynesian Omai, who had come to England aboard the *Adventure* and was now returning to the South Pacific with Cook, happily gave up his cabin to make room for the horses. "Nothing is wanting," Cook wrote, "but a few females of our own species to make the *Resolution* a compleate ark."

The vessels headed southeast so that Cook could verify some recently reported French sightings of land. On December 12 he came across a group of islands in the southern Indian Ocean that had been sighted by a Frenchman, Marion Du Fresne, four years earlier. Cook dubbed the group the Prince Edward Islands and named two nearby islets after

Impassive penguins ignore explorers from the Resolution and the Discovery, anchored off Kerguelen Island in the southern Indian Ocean. The absence of vegetation led Cook to describe Kerguelen as "naked and desolate in the highest degree." Hunters later made their way there with the aid of Cook's charts and exterminated the island's seal population.

Du Fresne and his deputy, Julien Marie Crozet. Two weeks later the *Resolution* and the *Discovery* hauled up at Kerguelen Island, which had eluded Cook in early 1773. The ships anchored in a rocky harbor on Christmas Day, 1776. The crew was given a day of rest, but it is not known whether Cook issued extra rations of liquor. Then Cook spent a week examining Kerguelen Island's desolate slopes and charting its deeply indented coast.

No sooner had Cook put out to sea than the *Resolution* began to labor in the subantarctic waters. In a sudden squall on January 19, 1777, she lost her fore-topmast and her main-topgallant mast. Cook carried a spare only for the fore-topmast. He stopped at Van Diemen's Land, cut some timber for the missing mast, then pressed on to New Zealand's Queen Charlotte's Sound, where he anchored on February 12, 1777. The resident Maoris feared he might take reprisals for the massacre of the *Adventure's* shore party three years before. But Cook assured them he intended no retribution.

He got away from New Zealand on February 27. The next destination in the *Resolution's* itinerary was Tahiti, en route to the North American coast. But Cook had fallen behind schedule and, realizing that the voyage was going to take longer than he had thought, decided to postpone the visit to Tahiti and refresh instead in the Tongas. The expedition arrived there on April 28 and remained for 11 weeks, visiting several of the islands and being welcomed with ceremonial dances, boxing matches and feasting. In return, the English treated the Tongans to a fireworks display and Marine drills.

Here Cook demonstrated that he was a changed man in two respects. Although the expedition had repeatedly received reports of the existence of several large islands to the north (they were, in fact, the Fijis and Samoa), Cook, to the astonishment of those veteran sailors who recalled his insatiable curiosity on his first two voyages, showed no interest in visiting them. Secondly, Cook's patience in the face of thievery had worn thin, and his passion for evenhanded treatment of islanders was now tarnished by a rage toward those he considered unrepentant. In the Tongas he not only had pilferers flogged but had crosses slashed on the arms of hardened offenders.

Cook finally took leave of the Tongans on July 17; four weeks later he

Heroic epilogue to the mutiny on the "Bounty"

Standing coatless amid loyal crewmen in the ship's launch, Captain Bligh makes a last effort to dissuade mutineers from seizing the Bounty.

reached the Society Islands and Tahiti. There his welcome was typically cordial, and he stayed nearly four months. On one occasion Cook and Clerke caused a sensation when they mounted two of the horses brought from Capetown—the Tahitians had never before seen horses—and galloped along the beach. Another time, when Cook complained of severe rheumatic pains in his hips, a Tahitian chief sent him a bevy of 12 plump girls, who deftly massaged the captain until "they made my bones crack and a perfect Mummy of my flesh." To Cook's surprise, his pain temporarily vanished, but it was only a matter of days before it returned and his temper flared again. On the nearby island of Moorea, unable to retrieve a stolen goat, he personally directed a search party that burned houses and war canoes. A few days later on Huahine, confronted by the theft of a sextant, he ordered the guilty person's ears cut off, an act that he would have considered unthinkable in earlier years.

In early December, with Omai relocated on Huahine, Cook left the Society Islands and made north for the Equator. After crossing more than

Storytellers have not been kind to William Bligh, who—13 years after he sailed as a master with Cook—was the victim of the most celebrated mutiny in history while he was commanding H.M.S. *Bounty*. Those recounting the tale in print and on film have painted Bligh as a sadist against whom mutiny was inevitable. But in his own time, much of the public regarded him as hero rather than villain.

The mutiny was swift and bloodless. On the morning of April 28, 1789, 25 men led by First Mate Fletcher Christian seized control of the *Bounty* while she was on a South Pacific voyage to collect breadfruit trees for Britain's colonies in the Caribbean. The mutineers drove Bligh and 18 loyal crewmen over the side and into the ship's launch—a 23-foot cockleshell with six pairs of oars and a small sail.

Bligh had been allowed to take a compass, a sextant, the ship's log and some private papers, but not the ship's chronometer. He and his men had just four cutlasses, and their food amounted to 150 pounds of biscuit, 20 pounds of salt pork, 28 gallons of water, five quarts of rum and a few coconuts.

Bligh took the launch in to the dubiously named Friendly Islands nearby to seek food and water, but was driven off by the inhabitants, who stoned one of his men to death. Resolving to take no chances on another such hostile encounter, he put the men on a daily ration of two ounces of biscuit and a quarter pint of water each, and shaped a course for the nearest European settlement, a Dutch port on the island of Timor, almost 4,000 miles away.

Soon a fierce storm struck, dumping quantities of rain into the launch and lifting mountainous waves over the stern. For 15 days all were "forced to bail without intermission," Bligh recalled. "The little sleep we got was in the midst of water, and we constantly awoke with severe cramps and pains in our bones." At length the rains ceased, but the blazing sunshine that followed was almost as punishing.

For six weeks the half-starved company rowed and sailed. Their only respite was off the coast of Australia, where Bligh allowed his men to go ashore on an apparently uninhabited island long enough to gather some oysters and berries. Timor was finally reached on June 14—without the loss of a single man other than the one stoned by the Friendly Islanders.

Bligh's return to England caused a sensation. The Admiralty, hearing his testimony and scrutinizing his log, promptly gave him command of another ship. The public approved, sharing the sentiment of the *Gentleman's Magazine*, which asserted: "The distresses he has undergone entitle him to every reward."

The verdict of history seems to be that Bligh was human enough, possessing both good and bad traits of character. Coolheaded and steadfast in an emergency but a petty tyrant in the humdrum work of a routine voyage, he excited passions that ranged from adulation to slander.

Because the mutiny succeeded at first—and mutinies rarely do—storytellers favored the perpetrators and obscured the virtues of this consummate seaman and forceful leader of men. In any event, Bligh himself felt justice had been done: All but one of the mutineers either were court-martialed, perished in a shipwreck, or were killed by Polynesians or by one another.

1,100 miles of open ocean, he sighted a small, uninhabited island on December 24. In observance of the holiday, he named his latest discovery Christmas Island, but again did not record in his log how the day was celebrated. Steering north, he was startled on January 18, 1778, to come on three large volcanic islands that appeared on none of his charts. They were the northwestern trio of the group now known as the Hawaiian Islands: Kauai, Niihau and Oahu.

Incredibly, despite more than two and a half centuries of Pacific exploration, none of the Hawaiian Islands had ever been seen by Europeans. Sailing closer to inspect the land, Cook discovered that the inhabitants, who came out to the ships in handsome canoes, spoke a Polynesian dialect similar to Tahitian.

He went ashore briefly on Kauai and got another surprise: Everywhere he went, people fell flat on their faces before him. Cook was astonished by this display of homage but, after puzzling over the matter, decided it was only their mode of paying respect to their "great chiefs." At Niihau Cook obtained some provisions and heard about other islands, some even larger, to the southeast. But he was anxious to reach the coast of North America early in the spring, and on February 2, after naming the group the Sandwich Islands after the First Lord of the Admiralty, he left.

From the central hut in this scene, Captain Cook and Tongan Chief Mariwaggy watch ceremonial mock fights during the explorers' 11-week visit to the Friendly Islands in 1777. The teepee-like structures at left and right in the clearing are stacks of skewered yams given to the English by the Tongans.

*Seated Tahitian priests petition their
god of war to grant victory in exchange for
their offering of a man, whose grave is
being dug near his corpse. Cook and two
other Englishmen (right) look on as
a dog is singed free of hair before being
added to the pile of dogs and pigs
already on the raised sacrificial altar.*

In his journal, Cook speculated that his new discovery might be "the most important that had hitherto been made by Europeans throughout the extent of the Pacific Ocean." He also praised the Hawaiians; observing that "no people could trade with more honisty: some indeed at first betrayed a thievish disposition, but this conduct they soon laid aside."

From Hawaii to North America the ocean was empty. Cook saw the "long looked for" headlands of the coast of present-day Oregon on March 7. Then, as he steered north, the weather closed in, and a westerly gale with heavy snow squalls lashed the ships for more than a week, driving them 120 nautical miles southward. When visibility returned, he clawed back to the north and made for a good harbor on a mountainous coast: It was Nootka Sound, on what is now Vancouver Island, British Columbia. There the expedition was forced to remain for a full month, making extensive repairs to the chronically weak *Resolution*, which required new rigging and an entire new mizzenmast.

Ashore, the English witnessed the ceremonial dances and the harmonious singing of the swarthy, dirt-encrusted Nootka Indians, who lived in communal log-framed houses adorned with fantastic wood carvings. Cook had his sailors row him around on inspection tours of the sound. One midshipman, James Trevenen, recalled later that "Captain Cooke on these occasions would sometimes relax from his almost constant severity of disposition, & condescend now and then to converse familiarly with us. But it was only for the time. As soon as we entered the ships, he became again the despot."

At the end of April, with the Indians singing a farewell, Cook resumed his survey of the American coast. The shoreline—replete with bays, headlands and peaks on which he freely bestowed names—stretched on and on. There was no passage to the east. One large gulf seemed promising, but after 150 miles it ended, hemmed in on all sides by snow-capped mountains; it would later be named Cook Inlet, and on its greatest harbor the city of Anchorage now stands.

As the ships pushed on, the coast turned to the southwest. The expedition reached the Aleutians on June 15, 1778. Cook found a passage through the fogbound island chain and sailed north again, into the Bering Sea. On August 9 he rounded the westernmost tip of America. He named the point Cape Prince of Wales and crossed the Bering Strait to the mainland of Asia, where he landed briefly before continuing his northern voyage.

The *Resolution* and the *Discovery* crossed the Arctic Circle on August 14, 1778, and once again Cook found himself negotiating hazardous ice floes. On August 18 the ships reached lat. 70° 44', where they were

Cook's men hunt "sea horses"— walruses—in ice-filled waters north of the Bering Strait. The explorers melted walrus blubber for lamp oil, reinforced their rigging with the skin and ate the meat. But Cook's claim that walrus fat tasted as "sweet as marrow" was disputed by his crew. "Captain Cook speaks entirely from his own taste," said one man, "surely the coarsest that ever mortal was endued with."

Believing Cook to be the long-awaited god Lono, Hawaiians carry propitiatory offerings across Kealakekua Bay to the foreign ships. Swaddled in cloth at the stern of the canoe at right are wickerwork effigies of other deities.

stopped by a solid mass of ice, rising 10 to 12 feet above the water, that stretched as far as he could see. The pack ice drifted dangerously with the winds, at times threatening to pin the ships against the coast. Cook could see no possible passage to the north or east and hauled off to the southwest, toward the Siberian shore—where a northeast passage over the top of Asia to Europe might begin. But the ships ran up against more ice, and there was no way through. On August 29, Cook judged that the brief arctic summer was nearing an end, and he turned south, intending to come back the following summer and resume the search.

The Admiralty's instructions had presumed that he would winter on Siberia's Kamchatka Peninsula, 1,262 miles southwest of the Bering Strait, but Cook chose instead to return to the Sandwich Islands. After stopping off in the Aleutians to mend the *Resolution's* leaks, he made south and arrived off the Sandwich group's largest island, Hawaii, in December. He spent almost six weeks cruising offshore and trading with Hawaiians who came out in boats. He postponed any landing in hopes of minimizing problems that contact with the islanders might bring. At last, on the morning of January 17, 1779, he came to anchor in "Karaka-kooa," or Kealakekua Bay, on Hawaii's western coast.

His welcome was tumultuous. More than 1,000 canoes, all filled with smiling, laughing Hawaiians, crowded around the ships, and many hundreds of swimmers came out from shore "like shoals of fish," according to one lieutenant. They swarmed up onto the ships and could be restrained only by their chiefs. Cook and his officers were treated with great deference. As on Kauai a year earlier, thousands of solemn natives prostrated themselves wherever Cook passed. That afternoon Cook, Clerke and several other Englishmen were conducted by priests to a shrine where the puzzled but compliant captain was wrapped in a sacred red cloth and anointed with various substances, to the accompaniment of a long series of incantations. Escorted back to the beach, he heard the word "Lono" being sounded repeatedly. What did it mean? What could account for the adoration?

Cook was the beneficiary—and victim—of an extraordinary coincidence. According to Hawaiian legend, a great god named Lono had left the islands many generations in the past but would one day return, bearing wonderful gifts. Each winter he was honored by processions of marchers who carried sacred staffs with banners attached to crosspieces as they followed a clockwise route around the island. Cook had come around the island at the appropriate moment in a clockwise direction, in ships whose masts, yards and sails corresponded to Lono's ceremonial staffs, crosspieces and white banners. Moreover, the iron nails, hatchets and knives that Cook exchanged for provisions were unlike any gifts the Hawaiians had ever received. Surely he was the deity incarnate.

A bearded Hawaiian wears a gourd mask with a foliage crest and dangling ribbons made from bark. Such masks figured in ceremonies devoted to Lono— an ancestral god who was expected to return to the islands some day and inaugurate an era of peace and abundance.

Cook knew none of this and could only marvel at the islanders' cordiality. He was presented with feathered capes and an extraordinary plumed helmet that resembled those of the ancient Greeks. Everywhere the visitors went they were treated as honored guests. Daily the islanders entertained the English with wrestling and dancing exhibitions, including performances of the hula. One officer noted the dexterity with which young Hawaiians used long planks to ride waves "with an incredible Swiftness to the shore"—perhaps the world's first account of surfing. Women thronged the ships. Food was plentiful, the island lovely.

After a fortnight the island chiefs began inquiring how long Cook expected to remain and subtly hinted that the English were overstaying their welcome. Apparently they had discovered reason to doubt his divinity. Sensing a change in the Hawaiians' mood, Cook announced that he would soon leave to visit the other islands. With repairs completed, the ships departed on February 4 for Maui. At this moment fate intervened cruelly. The English ships had not sailed more than a few miles when a storm came up and the foremast of the battered *Resolution* was sprung. The damage required immediate attention, and after no other anchorage could be found, Cook reluctantly returned to Kealakekua Bay, "all hands much chagrin'd & damning the Foremast."

The mood of the Hawaiians had indeed changed. Some had decided Cook was not Lono after all, and the English were no longer venerated. Thefts, which had been almost nonexistent in earlier weeks, now became a major problem. When caught, pilferers taunted the English. Diplomatically, Cook informed the Hawaiian priests that he planned to leave as soon as the *Resolution's* foremast could be repaired. On February 13 the weakened spar was unstepped and taken ashore, where the carpenters set to work with all possible speed. But the Hawaiians' regard for the English had deteriorated even faster. On the afternoon of February 13 a watering party from the *Discovery* was attacked by a stone-throwing crowd. When informed of the incident, Cook ordered that sentries' muskets henceforth be loaded not with small shot, which would only injure slightly, but with ball, which would kill. He was nearing the end of his patience.

That night the *Discovery's* cutter was stolen. Upon learning of the theft at 6 a.m. the following morning, Cook was livid. His anger, so long pent-up, exploded. Arming himself with a double-barreled musket— one barrel with small shot, the other with ball—he went ashore with a detachment of Marines to find the local chieftain and hold him hostage until the cutter was returned. He also ordered that canoes be prevented from leaving the bay. On shore, he went to the chief's house to persuade the old man to accompany him to the *Resolution*. The chief agreed and walked back to the beach with Cook. There the Hawaiian leader's wife and two lesser dignitaries begged him not to go, and he sat down, somewhat frightened. A crowd had gathered, armed with spears and stones.

In this romantic rendering of the death of James Cook, the explorer lies in the foreground, his eyes showing pain and disbelief, while a half-fallen Marine (left) stops a dagger-brandishing Hawaiian with a musket ball. Some of the daggers used against Cook's company had been acquired by the Hawaiians through trade with their English visitors.

An ambitious French venture that came to grief

The last major probe of the South Seas in the 18th Century was led by Jean-François de Galaup de La Pérouse, a redoubtable French nobleman and military hero whom King Louis XVI sent to the Pacific in 1785 to search for "all the lands that had escaped the vigilance of Cook."

A truly royal prodigality was exercised in preparing for the voyage. Some 20 artisans and scientists were engaged, and La Pérouse was given two 500-ton frigates, the *Astrolabe* and the *Boussole,* crammed with books, charts, and special supplies—including 10 reams of paper for pressing leaves to bring home, 20 barrels of water specifically for studying the growth of bacteria, and one million assorted pins to help win the friendship of any indigenous peoples the explorers might meet.

In two and a half years of almost constant sailing, La Pérouse described three vast loops through the Pacific, more or less retracing Cook's routes but proceeding farther, to such exotic outposts as Tatary (China and Siberia) and Japan. All along the way he wrote about his discoveries—detailing the lay of the land, noting anthropometric measurements of the peoples he encountered, and describing their food, clothing, houses and customs. His last stop was Cook's Botany Bay in Australia, where, obeying what must have been a prophetic impulse, he persuaded British colonial officers to transmit his letters and ship's log to Paris.

After he sailed from Botany Bay in February 1788, La Pérouse and his men were never heard from again. Their fate remained a mystery until the 1820s, when an Irish merchant visiting the Santa Cruz Islands happened upon a sword guard inscribed J.F.G.P. (the initials of Jean-François de Galaup de La Pérouse). From islanders who had been children at the time, he pieced together a story of shipwreck; they had some relics of the expedition, among them a ship's bell and several brass guns. The subsequent discovery of 60 European skulls gave grisly testimony that La Pérouse and his men had been killed and eaten by Santa Cruz Islanders—descendants of the same ferocious folk who had attacked would-be colonists led by Spanish explorers Mendaña and Quirós some 200 years earlier.

The British officers, true to their word, delivered La Pérouse' papers to France. That collection, published in 1797 as *Voyage round the World,* was a four-volume assortment of plates, charts and commentaries that provided a worthy finale to the era of Pacific navigation.

Jean-François de La Pérouse unrolls an explorer's map of the Pacific for Louis XVI (seated), as one of the King's ministers looks on.

Cook signaled his men to retreat and moved toward his boat. Just then the crowd received word that Englishmen elsewhere on the bay had killed another chief—the result of Cook's order to prevent canoes from leaving. Almost simultaneously a Hawaiian threatened Cook with a dagger. Cook fired his barrel of small shot at him, but the assailant, protected by a war mat, was unharmed and yelled defiance. The crowd began advancing. Cook fired his other barrel and killed a man. He yelled, "Take to the boats!" But he never got there himself. Knocked down, he was stabbed and held underwater, then stabbed again and again. Four Marines were also killed before the rest escaped. In shock, the survivors rowed silently back to the ships, leaving the dead behind. It was 8 a.m.

A stunned Charles Clerke succeeded to the command. Wisely, he decided against vengeance. Among the Hawaiians there was grief equaling that of the visitors: The terrible incident was a ghastly aberration in the islanders' normal behavior. In a few days a priest brought parts of Cook's body to the ship; he had been cut up and his flesh burned, but—as with any great chieftain—his bones had been preserved as relics. Clerke committed them to the bay, while 10 guns sounded a salute.

Clerke could have sailed straight home, but as a tribute to Cook he chose to continue the voyage. That spring, after a stop at Kamchatka, the ships sailed north through the Bering Strait and were again barred by the implacable ice. Defeated, they returned to Kamchatka. There Clerke, who had been suffering all through the voyage from tuberculosis, died. Lieutenant John Gore took over and brought the ships back to England. They arrived on October 4, 1780.

The news of Cook's death had preceded them, for Clerke had sent word from Kamchatka via the Russians. There had been genuine mourning, but it was short-lived: Britain was increasingly preoccupied with the war against its colonists across the Atlantic, which was going badly. Furthermore, it was difficult for most 18th Century Britons to understand the magnitude of Cook's achievements. Much of what he had done was, in a way, negative: He had proved that the fabled Southern continent did not exist, and he had shown that there was at least no warm-water Northwest Passage. The positive feats could be adequately appreciated only by later generations.

His associates, however, were well aware of his greatness. Lord Palliser, Cook's superior in the Navy, called him "the ablest and most renowned navigator this or any country hath produced. He possessed all the qualifications requisite for his profession and great undertakings." David Samwell, surgeon of the Discovery, wrote that Cook was "vigilant and active in an eminent degree; cool and intrepid among dangers; patient and firm under difficulties and distress; fertile in expedients; great and original in all his designs; active and resolved in carrying them into execution. In every situation he stood unrivalled and alone; on him all eyes were turned; he was our leading-star."

Other explorers understood too. In the opinion of the French navigator Jean-François de Galaup de La Pérouse, Cook's work was so all-encompassing that there was little for his successors to do but admire it. What he had bequeathed to posterity was at once grand and simple: a coherent map of the Pacific.

Acknowledgments

The index for this book was prepared by Gale Linck Partoyan. The editors wish to thank the following: Gerard J. A. Raven, consultant; Dr. William Thomas Stearn, consultant *(pages 134-139)*; John Batchelor, artist, and David Lyon, consultant *(pages 109-111)*; Bill Hezlep, artist *(pages 35, 46, 58, 92, 114, 158)*; Peter McGinn, artist *(endpaper maps)*; Lloyd K. Townsend, artist, and Ben R. Finney, consultant *(pages 98-105)*.

The editors also wish to thank: In Australia: Canberra—Rex Nan Kivell Collection, Barbara Perry, Pictorial Librarian, National Library of Australia; Sydney—Dixon Library; Patricia Jackson, Suzanne Mourot, Librarian, Mitchell Library. In Denmark: Copenhagen—Palle Birkelund, Director, Henrik Stuhlmann, Manuscripts Department, Royal Library. In France: Paris—Jean-Paul Alaux; Philippe Henrat, Curator, Archives Nationales; Yves Laissus, Curator, Bibliothèque Centrale du Musée d'Histoire Naturelle; Edwige Archier, Curator, Departement des Cartes et Plans, Bibliothèque Nationale; Jean Boudriot; Sophie Amet, Musée des Arts Africains et Océaniens; Jean-Claude Jolinon, Laboratoire de Phanerogamie, Musée d'Histoire Naturelle; Hervé Cras, Director for Historical Studies, Marjolaine Mathikine, Librarian, Denise Chaussegroux, Researcher, Musée de la Marine; Kerbreho—Count François de Bougainville; Sèvres—Tamara Préaud, Archiviste, Manufacture Nationale de Sèvres; Vincennes—Jean Pierre Busson, Chief Curator, Gabriel Labar, Director of the Library, Janine Richet, Service Historique de la Marine. In the Netherlands: Amsterdam—Rijksmuseum; Rijksmuseum Nederlands Scheepvaart Museum; Alkmaar—Stedelijk Museum; The Hague—Algemeen Rijksarchief; Martin de Vries, Photographer; Hoorn—Westfries Museum; Leyden—Leyden University Library; Rotterdam—Atlas van Stolk. In New Zealand: Wellington—Anthony Murray-Oliver, Alexander Turnbull Library; Auckland—Professor Bruce Biggs, Professor of Maori Studies, University of Auckland. In Spain: Madrid—Don Fermín Muñoz, Secretary to the Duchess of Alba, Liria Palace; Don Jaime Jiménez, Museo Naval; Don Fernando Fuertes de Villaviciencio, Consejero Delegado Gerente, Patrimonio Nacional; Valladolid—Don Armando Represa, Director, Archivo de Simancas. In Tahiti: Papeete—Société des Études Océaniennes. In the United Kingdom: London—John Huddy, British Library; Dr. P.J.P. Whitehead, Senior Principal Scientific Officer, A. C. Wheeler, Principal Scientific Officer, Department of Zoology, Anna Datta, Judith Diment, Caroline Whitefoord, R. Williams, British Museum; Dr. Wendy Baron, Dr. Mary Beal, Department of the Environment; Dr. Averil Lysaght; Dorota Czarkowska Starzecka, Assistant Keeper, Museum of Mankind; E.H.H. Archibald, Curator of Oil Paintings, Beresford Hutchinson, Curator of Astronomy, H. H. Preston, Curator of Prints and Drawings, Joan Moore, Roger Quarm, Stephen Riley, J. E. Tucker, National Maritime Museum; Jane Roundell.

The editors also wish to thank: In the United States: Washington, D.C.—Vondel Chamberlain, Chief, Presentations Division, National Air and Space Museum, Smithsonian Institution; John Lyall, Boyd Peterson, John G. Ulrich, Defense Mapping Agency and Hydrographic/Topographic Center; Dr. Estelle Irizarry, Professor of Spanish, Georgetown University; Thomas G. DeClaire, Gary Fitzpatrick, Reference Librarians, Geography and Map Division, Library of Congress; Trevor Hughes, Information Officer, Cultural Affairs, Annette Fitzpatrick, Information Assistant, New Zealand Embassy; Engrid Peters, Information Assistant, Royal Netherlands Embassy; Dr. P. M. Janiczek, Dr. Paul Routly, U.S. Naval Observatory; Cambridge, Massachusetts—Sally Bond, Archivist, The Peabody Museum of Archaeology and Ethnology, Harvard University; Honolulu, Hawaii—Dr. Kenneth P. Emory, Senior Anthropologist, Debra Sullivan, Assistant to the Photo Librarian, Bishop Museum; Kailua-Kona, Hawaii—Herb Kane; New York, New York—Edward Dodd, Dodd, Mead & Company; Sheila Curl, Rare Book Division, New York Public Library.

Valuable sources of quotations were *The Discovery of the Solomon Islands by Alvaro de Mendaña in 1568* by Lord Amherst of Hackney and Basil Thomson, The Hakluyt Society, 1901; *The Life of Captain James Cook* by J. C. Beaglehole, Stanford University Press, 1974; *The Voyages of Pedro Fernández de Quirós, 1595-1606* by Clements Markham, The Hakluyt Society, 1904; and *The Discovery of Australia* by G. Arnold Wood, Macmillan, 1969.

Bibliography

Allen, Edward, *The Vanishing Frenchman*. Charles E. Tuttle, 1959.

Amherst of Hackney, Lord, and Basil Thomson, *The Discovery of the Solomon Islands by Alvaro de Mendaña in 1568*. 2nd series, Vols. 7 and 8. London: Hakluyt Society, 1901.

Anderson, Bern, *The Life and Voyages of Captain George Vancouver*. University of Washington Press, 1960.

Beaglehole, J. C.:
The Exploration of the Pacific. 3rd ed. Stanford University Press, 1966.
The Life of Captain James Cook. Stanford University Press, 1974.

Beaglehole, J. C., ed.:
The Endeavour Journal of Joseph Banks, 1768-1771. 2 vols. Sydney: Angus & Robertson, 1962.
The Journals of Captain James Cook, Vols. 1, 2 and 3. Cambridge: Cambridge University Press, 1955.
The Voyage of the Resolution and Adventure, 1772-1775. Cambridge: Cambridge University Press, 1961.
The Voyage of the Resolution and Discovery, 1776-1780. Cambridge: Cambridge University Press, 1967.

Clissold, Stephen, *Conquistador: The Life of Don Pedro Sarmiento de Gamboa*. London: Derek Verschoyle, 1954.

Dahlgren, M.E.W., *Voyages Français à Destination de la Mer du Sud avant Bougainville*. Paris: Imprimerie Nationale, 1907.

Dampier, William, *A New Voyage round the World*. Dover, 1968.

De Villiers, J.A.J., *The East and West Indian Mirror Being an Account of Joris van Speilbergen's Voyage round the World (1614-1617) and the Australian Navigations of Jacob Le Maire*. London: Hakluyt Society, 1906.

Dodd, Edward, *Polynesian Seafaring*. Dodd, Mead, 1972.

Dodge, Ernest, *Beyond the Capes*. Little, Brown, 1971.

Dunmore, John, *French Explorers in the Pacific*, Vol. 1. Oxford: Oxford University Press, 1965.

Finney, Ben R., *Hokule'a: The Way to Tahiti*. Dodd, Mead, 1979.

Forster, John Reinhold, transl., *A Voyage round the World*. Da Capo Press, 1967.

Gay, Peter, *The Enlightenment: An Interpretation*. Knopf, 1973.

Gould, R. T., *Captain Cook*. London: Duckworth, 1978.

Hammond, L. David, ed., *News from New Cythera, 1766-1769*. University of Minnesota Press, 1970.

Heeres, J. E.:
Abel Janszoon Tasman's Journal. Amsterdam: Frederik Muller, 1898.
The Part Borne by the Dutch in the Discovery of Australia. London: Luzac, 1899.

Hough, Richard:
Captain Bligh and Mr. Christian. Lon-

don: Hutchinson, 1972.
The Last Voyage of Captain James Cook. William Morrow, 1979.

Inder, Stuart, ed., *Pacific Islands Year Book.* Pacific Publications, 1978.

Jack-Hinton, Colin, *The Search for the Islands of Solomon: 1567-1838.* Oxford: Clarendon Press, 1969.

Kahn, Robert, ed., *Georg Forsters Werke, A Voyage round the World.* Berlin: Akademie-Verlag, 1968.

Kelly, Celsus, *La Austrialia del Espíritu Santo.* 2 vols. Cambridge: Hakluyt Society, 1966.

Knight, Frank, *Captain Cook and the Voyage of the Endeavour (1768-1771).* Melbourne: Thomas Nelson, 1968.

Lee, Ida, *Captain Bligh's Second Voyage to the South Seas.* London: Longmans, Green, 1920.

Lettsom, John Coakley, ed., *A Journal of a Voyage to the South Seas, in His Majesty's Ship the Endeavour.* London: Papers of the late Sydney Parkinson, 1784.

Lewis, David, *The Voyaging Stars.* W. W. Norton, 1978.

Lloyd, Christopher, *Atlas of Maritime History.* Arco, 1975.

McCormick, E. H., *Omai, Pacific Envoy.* Auckland: Auckland University Press, 1977.

MacLean, Alistair, *Captain Cook.* Doubleday, 1972.

Markham, Clements, *The Voyages of Pedro Fernández de Quirós, 1595-1606.* 2nd series, Nos. 14 and 15. London: Hakluyt Society, 1904.

Parkinson, Sydney, *A Voyage to the South Seas aboard HMS Endeavour.* London: 1773.

Reed, A. W., ed.:
Captain Cook in Australia, Extracts from the Journals of Captain James Cook. Sydney: Halstead Press, 1969.
Captain Cook in New Zealand, Extracts from the Journals of Captain James Cook. Sydney: Halstead Press, 1969.

Rienits, Rex and Thea, *The Voyages of Captain Cook.* London: Hamlyn Publishing Group, 1968.

Roberts, Gail, *Atlas of Discovery.* Crown Publishers, 1973.

Ross, Michael, *Bougainville.* Gordon and Cremonesi Publishers, 1978.

Schouten, Willem Corneliszoon, *A Wonderfull Voiage round about the World.* Da Capo Press, 1968.

Sharp, Andrew, *The Voyages of Abel Janszoon Tasman.* Oxford: Clarendon Press, 1968.

Smith, Bernard, *European Vision and the South Pacific.* Oxford: Oxford University Press, 1960.

Taillemite, Étienne, *Bougainville et Ses Compagnons—Autour du Monde—1766-1769.* Paris: Imprimerie Nationale, 1977.

Thiery, Maurice, *Bougainville—Soldier and Sailor.* London: Grayson & Grayson, 1932.

Villiers, Alan, *Captain James Cook.* Charles Scribner's Sons, 1967.

Wallis, Helen, ed., *Carteret's Voyage round the World, 1766-1769.* Cambridge: Cambridge University Press, 1965.

Wood, G. Arnold:
The Discovery of Australia. Melbourne: Macmillan, 1969.
The Voyage of the Endeavour. Melbourne: Macmillan, 1926.

Picture Credits

Index

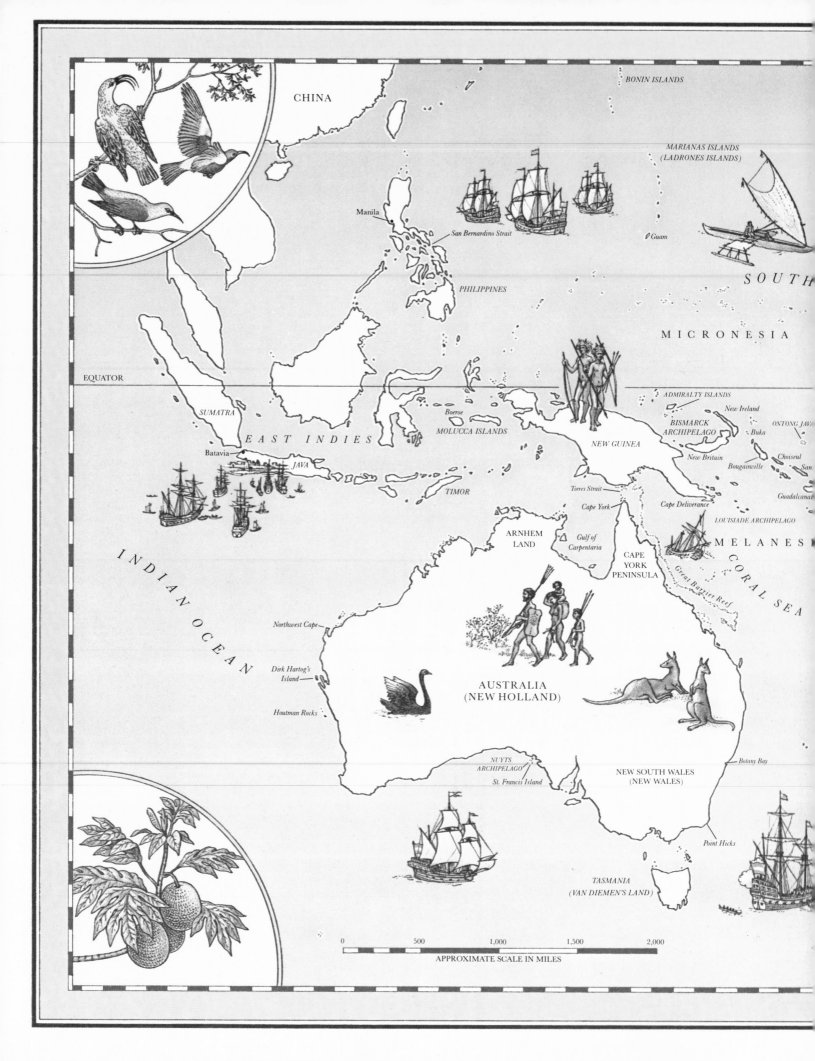

CHINA

BONIN ISLANDS

MARIANAS ISLANDS
(LADRONES ISLANDS)

Manila

San Bernardino Strait

Guam

PHILIPPINES

SOUTH

MICRONESIA

EQUATOR

SUMATRA

Boeroe

MOLUCCA ISLANDS

EAST INDIES

Batavia

JAVA

ADMIRALTY ISLANDS

New Ireland

BISMARCK
ARCHIPELAGO

ONTONG JAVA

Buka

NEW GUINEA

New Britain

Bougainville

Choiseul

San

Guadalcanal

TIMOR

Torres Strait

Cape York

Cape Deliverance

LOUISIADE ARCHIPELAGO

MELANES

INDIAN OCEAN

ARNHEM
LAND

Gulf of
Carpentaria

CAPE
YORK
PENINSULA

CORAL SEA

Great Barrier Reef

Northwest Cape

Dirk Hartog's
Island

Houtman Rocks

AUSTRALIA
(NEW HOLLAND)

NEW SOUTH WALES
(NEW WALES)

Botany Bay

NUYTS
ARCHIPELAGO

St. Francis Island

Point Hicks

TASMANIA
(VAN DIEMEN'S LAND)

0   500   1,000   1,500   2,000

APPROXIMATE SCALE IN MILES